"If anyone knows about the supernatural, Mickey Robinson certainly does. I heartily recommend this book to you!"

Eric Metaxas, *New York Times* bestselling author
and host of the *Eric Metaxas Radio Show*

"Get ready to embrace fresh, living hope empowered by the Holy Spirit as you read Mickey Robinson's new book. *Supernatural Courage* is full of astounding testimonies of God's love and power, and I believe it will impart spiritual courage so you can take hold of the promises of God with renewed purpose."

Dr. Ché Ahn, founder and president of Harvest International Ministry and international chancellor of Wagner University

"Mickey Robinson's life and ministry exemplify supernatural courage. By reading Mickey's new book, you can equip yourself with the very same courage that the greatest men and women of the Bible used to achieve God's ultimate plan for their lives and to transform the lives of others. If you want to take your life to the next level and stand up to the greatest challenges this world offers, learn and follow the principles laid out in *Supernatural Courage*, and you'll never be the same!"

Jordan Rubin, *New York Times* bestselling author
of *The Maker's Diet* and founder
of Garden of Life and Ancient Nutrition

"Since the Garden of Eden, God has been searching for individuals with the courage to trust Him thoroughly. Mickey's life has been all about such courage as God has led him from a life-threatening accident, through miraculous personal healing and into a life of powerful ministry. This book imparts the wisdom he has gained about true Christian courage. Read it with expectation—this same God wants to encourage you."

Michael S. Brooks, M.D.

"It takes courage to be human. We are subject, because of the original Fall, to weaknesses, frailties, vulnerabilities and even death.

Mickey is as human as you can be from a Scriptural perspective. He is as real and as vulnerable as it gets. In my opinion, that is what makes *Supernatural Courage* so appealing. Mickey shows us how to be courageously human by the power of the Holy Spirit!"

Dr. Mark J. Chironna, founder of Mark Chironna Ministries and founding and lead pastor of Church On The Living Edge, Longwood, Florida

"Here's a book you need to read, especially in the days we're living in! There is no one I can think of more suited to write a book about supernatural courage than Mickey Robinson. He has given us a deep well to swim in to find the measure of courage to live for God in this difficult time. You will be baptized into fresh courage just by reading this book!"

Brian Simmons, The Passion Translation Project

"Mickey Robinson's extraordinary, personal, supernatural courage allows him to write with an authenticity and authority that will impart supernatural courage to every reader. Learn from an expert and increase your own supernatural courage. You can. You must!"

Steve Berger, founding pastor of Grace Chapel, Franklin, Tennessee

"Do you want to grow in your faith and be more courageous in your life? Do you believe there are giants in the land that you need to conquer? Is there a new territory you need to take? If so, Mickey Robinson's book *Supernatural Courage* will feed your soul and inspire your heart to be an overcomer in Christ Jesus. You are destined for greatness! So follow the life example and the courageous ministry of one of my most trusted friends in the Body of Christ. You were born to come out on the other side better than you came in!"

James W. Goll, author, international speaker and founder of God Encounters Ministries and GOLL Ideation

SUPERNATURAL COURAGE /////////////

SUPERNATURAL
COURAGE

///

ACTIVATING SPIRITUAL BRAVERY TO WIN TODAY'S BATTLE

MICKEY ROBINSON

Chosen
a division of Baker Publishing Group
Minneapolis, Minnesota

© 2020 by Michael Robinson

Published by Chosen Books
11400 Hampshire Avenue South
Bloomington, Minnesota 55438
www.chosenbooks.com

Chosen Books is a division of
Baker Publishing Group, Grand Rapids, Michigan

Printed in the United States of America

Library of Congress Cataloging-in-Publication Data
Names: Robinson, Mickey, author.
Title: Supernatural courage : activating spiritual bravery to win today's battle / Mickey
   Robinson.
Description: Minneapolis, Minnesota : Chosen Books, 2020. | Includes bibliographical
   references.
Identifiers: LCCN 2019050414 | ISBN 9780800799595 (trade paper) | ISBN 9781493422982
   (ebook)
Subjects: LCSH: Courage—Religious aspects—Christianity. | Fear—Religious Aspects—
   Christianity. | Spiritual warfare—Prayers and devotions.
Classification: LCC BV4647.C75 .R63 2020 | DDC 241/.4—dc23
LC record available at https://lccn.loc.gov/2019050414

Cover design by Studio Gearbox

20 21 22 23 24 25 26   7 6 5 4 3 2 1

I dedicate this book to
Barbara Ann Robinson
and Anne Severance.
You both are Spirit-empowered women
who hold a special place of honor and strength
among the saints.

CONTENTS

FOREWORD

Not everyone would attempt to jump out of an airplane on a skydiving expedition at 12,500 feet, but our dear friend Mickey did as a brash nineteen year old. Call that bold and adventurous! Call it courageous! Call it just an extreme and borderline reckless choice in that time of his life! But what emerged from his boyhood brush with death when the plane crashed one August day was a supernatural brand of courage that has inspired, encouraged and challenged audiences around the world. And now we have a book that gives us the secret to attaining that kind of courage for ourselves.

We may not opt for skydiving as a hobby, but we live in a dangerous world. We are surrounded by constant threats—terrorism, fatal diseases, accidents, drugs and, always, the evil intent of our archenemy, Satan. Through these and other means, his agenda is to take us out or, at the very least, to render us helpless and hopeless. That is where this book comes in.

In eleven powerful chapters, Mickey carves out the path to bold, brave living. As a trailblazing overcomer through his neardeath experience, he weaves his own story of God's redeeming love throughout the steps to victorious living—courage to hope, to follow Jesus, to be humble, to fight, to strengthen yourself, to persevere, to use your gifts, to succeed, to forgive, to love and to go the distance.

With humility and transparency, Mickey confesses his own fears and inadequacies and reveals how God has walked him through the deepest valleys and helped him soar to the mountaintops through the empowering of the Holy Spirit. In each chapter, Mickey profiles another courageous person—a biblical hero or someone Mickey knows personally—who was able to overcome an "impossible" situation with God's supernatural strength.

During the writing of this book, Mickey and his fearless, gifted wife, Barbara, faced the challenge of their lives when she was diagnosed with stage IV cancer. Testing their courage to the deepest level yet, the Lord took them and many of those who love them to the throne of grace. Walking through this trial with them was a privilege for us—crying out to our Father in prayer and worship, drawing us closer to Him and to each other.

We have walked through life with Mickey for twenty years. We have ministered together, laughed and cried together, and prayed and worshiped in seasons of victories and struggles, and we all know from experience that it is not about what *we* can achieve with our own natural talents and abilities. Let me, Michael, be honest with you. When I am behind a keyboard, worshiping the Lord, I feel more than seven feet tall. I could never do what I do without the supernatural anointing of the Holy Spirit. Neither can Mickey—and neither can you! As Mickey famously says, "Jesus doesn't call us to what we *can* do, but to what we *can't* do without Him." That takes supernatural courage.

Michael W. and Debbie Smith

ACKNOWLEDGMENTS

To David Sluka and the Chosen publishing family, thanks for all of your patience and ongoing support throughout this project. My hope is that this work would more than meet our expectation to encourage, inspire and activate the lives of its readers. I pray that it brings light in their relationships and strength in their inner circles.

Anne Severance, you are not only a premier wordsmith with a special craft for writing and giving expert advice, you are also a true friend and servant of the Lord. You brought me light and warmth in a severe time of darkness.

Barbara, you have been a source of courage, even in the face of death, while I struggled to finish this book.

To the contributors Joe Bradford, Jordan Christy, Jordan Rubin, Reimar Schultze and Dr. Don Finto, I am truly grateful. Bill and Noni Butler, thank you for standing strong with us on a daily basis. Dennis and Susan Freeman, your love is as solid as Georgian Bay granite. Henry and Betsy Headden and our Acts 13 prayer gatherings, you are frontline, passionate intercessors and lovers of Jesus who have continuously poured life into me all of these years—especially the last twelve months.

I am grateful for the multitude of people who have been praying for us during this time as Barbara was blindsided with stage

IV cancer and subsequently had dangerous emergency surgery and treatment to walk out her healing. Jordan and Nicki Rubin, you have given selflessly of your time, your expertise in healing wisdom, your prayers and your strength.

I am grateful to my children and grandchildren: Michael, Matt and Natasha, and Solomon. Jake and Sommer, Elijah, Shiloh and Jorden, Bryan and Elizabeth, Ariel, Merci and Ivy. I have never been more grateful and jealous for your well-being and success. You, more than anybody, will be my testimony and legacy. I am profoundly aware of your love.

To the reader, I hope not only that you enjoy this book but also that something will happen in you to activate a new passion for Jesus. I pray that you will be bold in your expression, that you will have the courage to try something new and that you will fan the flame of the Holy Spirit to maintain a "burning heart." I am convinced now more than ever that the Body of our Lord Jesus Christ has profound power through prayer. This awareness has been acutely sharp throughout the process of writing this manuscript. "As you help us by means of your prayers for us. So it will be that the many prayers for us will be answered, and God will bless us; and many will raise their voices to him in thanksgiving for us" (2 Corinthians 1:11 GNT).

There are so many more people that I need to acknowledge that I am actually overwhelmed at the thought of the beauty and sincerity of all who have reached out to us during all this time. I will have to find some way in my inadequacy to thank and honor them. "Rejoice always, pray without ceasing, in everything give thanks; for this is the will of God in Christ Jesus for you" (1 Thessalonians 5:16–18).

INTRODUCTION

Spoiler alert: You will not need courage when you are in heaven. Reality check: You are not in heaven yet. Genuine followers of Jesus who have surrendered their lives to His Lordship will encounter circumstances and events that require spiritual bravery throughout their earthly walk.

If you are facing a challenge and are looking for answers, I believe that there are keys within this book that will speak to you. The Holy Spirit will help you rise above your circumstances to walk in victory. Everybody admires a true hero, whether that person is an incredible underdog like young David challenging Goliath, or Mary Magdalene who dared to go to Jesus' tomb (against all of society's rules) and was the first to see the risen Lord.

In these chapters, you will read about them and other biblical characters who found the courage to overcome obstacles. I hope you will enjoy reading their stories. I also include testimonies of modern-day heroes—many of whom I know personally. Through these stories and some of my own experiences, you will see that it takes guts to break through into glory. More than that, however, I want you to realize that Christ, the hope of glory, is in you, and He can write the very best stories through you.

The Lord refers to His people as His sheep. You are not, however, called to be sheepish. He has not given you a spirit of timidity;

instead, He gave you a spirit of love, power and a sound mind (see 2 Timothy 1:7). The more you respond with spiritual bravery to the issues in your life, the more you will develop a redemptive rhythm. Identity, purpose and vision are all modern-day themes that require a work of the Spirit to enable you to walk bravely on the path that is laid out before you. I believe that your senses are sharpened by engaging and cooperating with the Holy Spirit as you navigate within God's boundaries.

Actually, courage is not an option—it is a commandment: "Have I not commanded you? Be strong and of good courage; do not be afraid, nor be dismayed, for the LORD your God is with you wherever you go" (Joshua 1:9). In fact, three times within four verses we are admonished to be brave.

Some might ask, "What is coming that would lead me to need all of this bravery?" Joshua gives us a hint to the answer: "For you have not passed this way before" (Joshua 3:4). As it was in Joshua's day, it is now. As the darkness deepens around us, we do not have a pattern to follow; rather, we are to follow after the presence of the Lord. The Lord always leads us in triumph—but it still takes courage to get there.

In chapter 1, I share a short sketch of my testimony. I hope that my story displays clearly my weakness and God's incredible power. It is a testimony of hope from someone who was actually hopeless. I required supernatural courage on a regular basis, whether it was in the process of making little decisions or encountering difficult circumstances. I had to walk where I had never walked before.

We are all called to report for active duty to the Lord and His purposes. I hope sincerely that you are strengthened with power in your inner being as you actively engage in God's plan for your life. As a spiritual pilgrim, you have the ability to take others with you as you experience the unfolding promises of God. As you are willing, He is able to guide you safely to His intended destination.

CHAPTER 1 //

COURAGE TO HOPE

Hope is a golden cord connecting you to heaven.

Sarah Young, *Jesus Calling*

Everybody needs supernatural, spiritual courage to enter the Kingdom of God and to walk by faith. We need courage daily to meet life's challenges with grace, love and patience. Experiencing a true encounter with God changes everything. One of the most powerful aspects of a genuine God encounter is that it generates hope. Not a whimsical, wishful, maybe-if hope, but a dynamic expectancy that God is going to do something that is beyond the natural abilities found in this visible world.

How could anybody be qualified to assert such a lofty opinion? Only through living a life where the idea of false bravado and bravery was chipped repetitively away, and where traditional ideas of what courage is were confronted in substantial ways. In my life, attempts at bravery fell victim to the reality of trauma and tragedy. Let me tell you about myself and how my early life experiences led to my first real encounter with supernatural courage.

I was born in 1949 and was raised in Independence, Ohio, which was an ideal middle-to-upper-class community. The era was one in which it felt like the American dream was attainable by anybody.[1] I grew up in the first television generation, where everything about achievement was presented as positive and desirable. Despite some early hindrances in my life—in the first grade, I was laughed at for mispronouncing a few words while reading out loud, and consequently, I developed a stutter—I began playing and excelling in team sports. My innate athletic ability and ease in making friends fueled my desire to improve myself, and with time I was able to overcome the stammering. The 1950s in America was a golden time to fulfill dreams.

Yet my earliest memories also held dark secrets. My father was an alcoholic, and that brought me both fear and shame. Even though I had two older sisters and a younger brother, I was singled out and picked on by him. (That might have been because I was the first male born in our family.)

I have no recollection of ever hearing him say a single nice thing to me. I never heard things like "You did a good job at baseball, son," or "I like your friends," or "I love you." Every holiday ended with volatile domestic meltdowns. I grew up not wanting to be anything like my dad—the way he dressed, the way he spoke or the friends he chose.

Consequently, I threw myself into sports and social activities. Each endeavor I ventured into required the courage to succeed. I continued to improve in football, which I had played since second grade. I was first in my class to become an expert snow skier. I did very well in the performing arts, and during my senior year, I won an acting award at a state competition. I learned gymnastics on my own and did physical things no one in the history of our school had ever attempted. I thought I was doing it for the fun of it, but I now realize that other motives were beneath my feverish drive.

Besides schoolwork and sports practices, I held down a job that allowed me to become more and more independent. Eventually I was able to buy my own car, clothes and sports equipment. This allowed me to craft my own image. I talked my way into a dream job in an upscale brokerage firm when I was eighteen. Even after receiving a promotion in a promising career, I made a reckless decision after having been tempted by a friend. Part of the fallout from that bad decision was that my desire for the business world dissipated. While I thought that I was burying all of those bad feelings, I did not realize that I was burying them alive.

Falling into Freedom?

Love for aviation started as a fascination early in my childhood with the fictional hero Superman. I studied and memorized the history of flight—ballooning, gliders, the Wright brothers, Lindbergh, World War I and II aircraft, NASA and the space program.

This desire to fly would totally dominate and consume my life. I responded to an ad for a five-dollar flying lesson. From my first flight, it was obvious I was a natural. I loved absolutely everything about being in the sky.

The Cleveland Sportsman Show was a large annual event. Shortly after learning how to fly, I went to the show to take a look at a tiny do-it-yourself helicopter I had seen demonstrated in a James Bond movie. James Bond was my kind of guy. Although I knew it was all fantasy, he modeled a pretty fabulous life.

Before I could find the Bensen Gyrocopter display, I encountered the skydiving exhibit. After my first time jumping from a plane, I was smitten. Every flying adventure I had ever dreamed of culminated in the sensation of skydiving. What a rush! After twenty jumps, I was invited to join a professional skydiving team. I was considered an elite skydiver, and nothing else mattered to me.

I lived for the moment with little or no concern for the consequences and no thought of the future. Every new challenge required me to be courageous and bold—whether to be brave enough to do something for the first time or simply to have the tenacity to keep getting better. It was all part of the training and honing of my natural skills and talents that was required to be able to operate on higher levels. For me, the pinnacle was the satisfaction of being a free-fall artist and a skilled parachutist.

The courage to operate successfully in a high-risk sport was also an escape from life's problems. Free fall was the ultimate escape, falling into freedom jump after jump. I had adapted myself to be able to find pleasure only when living for the moment. I was blinded by the obsession. The desire for the next "fix" was insatiable. There would never be enough to satisfy.

Mayday! Mayday!

On a hot August evening, five skydivers loaded into the six-passenger modified Piper aircraft. Dan, Steve and I were professionals. Rick and Johnny were students. The two rookies would be jumping at lower altitudes, and that took a lot of extra time. The delay annoyed me. I was eager to go all the way to the top floor for the longest free-fall moment of my life. As the wheels came off the ground, I closed my eyes and settled back in my seat to wait out the long flight so that I could get my free-fall fix. Suddenly—silence.

The engine quit.

There was no time to leap to safety before the right wing on my side of the aircraft crashed into a tree. We violently cartwheeled and then plunged into the ground. At a dizzying speed, my face smashed into the instrument panel on impact. In the confusion, Steve helped the two students out of the mangled fuselage. My partner, Dan, had already exited and was a few feet away when the plane exploded. When he heard my screams, he rushed back to the wreckage. With superhuman effort, he extracted me—soaked in airplane fuel and on fire from head to toe.

As the ambulance raced to the nearest hospital, this overconfident young buck cried out to a God I did not know—to the Lord I had never served. "Please, God. I'm sorry! Help me! Please, help me!" Drifting into shock and not really knowing the extent of my injuries, this desperate cry was my first sincere prayer. It started something new—an authentic hope for God's help.

After arriving at the hospital, a triage team took over quickly. My injuries were catastrophic. Although I was young and strong—a professional athlete in my prime—the doctors did not think I would make it through the night. Severe third-degree burns covered a large portion of my body. I had a brain contusion from the blunt force of my head hitting the instrument panel. I was blind in my right eye with the skin burned off my retracted eyelids. Some of the most severe burns had seared my face, my right hand and arm, all of my right leg, and the back of my left leg. The flames had penetrated the muscle almost to the bone.

The next day in intensive care several close family members and friends were allowed to see me. I know now they were being advised to say their good-byes. Even though my situation was thought to be hopeless the doctors and nurses worked heroically in an attempt to save my life.

Although feverish efforts were exerted to prevent additional problems, I developed several potentially fatal complications. Massive infection spread over the outside of my body. In a few weeks my finely tuned athletic body withered to 93 pounds. I was losing ten pints of blood on some days. The blood became infected, and the nerves in the front part of my legs died. The lower portion of my esophagus was being eaten up by acid, and it was impossible for any nourishment to pass through to my stomach. My body cavity became septic. At this point, an expert consulting physician was asked to come in from a famous medical school.

At the end of his diagnostic summary, he wrote, "There is nothing I can offer this young man." The downward spiral of deadly complications was at the point of irreversibility. No scientific or medical treatment would help. As all my bodily functions were shutting down, there was absolutely no hope. They intended to continue with fluids and pain medicine until the mercy of death brought me relief.

When All Hope Was Gone

As my life was ebbing away and I was at the end stage, my spirit was expelled suddenly from my body, and I appeared in a spiritual dimension. In this realm, I had a revelation of the magnitude of eternity that is impossible to experience through your five senses.

Traveling on an upward path to a pure white circular portal, I felt a pressure on my right. As I turned to see what the pressure was, I found myself staring into a vast blackness. It, too, was eternal—eternal separation from the Source of all life. In this sphere was permanent solitary confinement—unimaginable, nonnegotiable and final. This realm is called the outer darkness.

I cried out a desperate plea with my spirit: *God, I'm sorry! Give me another chance, please! I want to live!*

Before the darkness could engulf me, I was thrust through the portal and into the very presence of God in what is called the third heaven. I comprehended instantly a new reality: I am a spirit. This is the true essence of our inner being. The river of life was coursing through my spirit-being, and I knew that I would never die—ever.

I perceived myriads of wonders and experienced the shock and awe of God's love and care for me that extends throughout eternity. Words cannot describe the power, the glory and the immeasurable, undiluted, perfect love of God. In a heavenly vision, I was shown the near future that extended about six years. All of these realizations happened before I was sent back to the natural, physical world.

My spirit reentered my shattered, broken body; however, the majestic Lord entered in with me. Though it was apparent to the medical staff that I had been spared death's grip at least temporarily they were still expecting me to die at any moment. The Source of all life began empowering me by the healing love of Jesus, Lord of even the impossible. The same Spirit that raised Jesus from the dead was inside my mortal body.

The doctors were at first skeptical, then stunned, and then determined to work with this phenomenon that they did not understand—a patient alive in a condition beyond medical comprehension. The trickle of healing not anticipated in the medical books was a result of my spiritual transformation.

I, of course, had never experienced anything remotely like this. The most astounding reality was the amazing love of God and the peace that resided in me that defied psychological description. But this is exactly what Scripture promises when it says, "The peace of God, which surpasses all understanding, will guard your hearts and minds through Christ Jesus" (Philippians 4:7).

Jesus—My Living Hope

A few weeks after my near-death experience and glorious heavenly encounter, my body was awaking from the grip of death—but so was the awful sensation of pain.

"Mr. Robinson, we need to move you to change your bed," one of the evening-shift nurses said.

"Oh, please . . . not now. I don't feel well tonight," I said in a weak whisper.

"It's okay. It won't take long," the nurse insisted, her voice trailing off.

Unable to find a male orderly, four female nurses each took one corner of the sheet to lift me off the bed and into a wheelchair. They raised me slowly up over the bed rails and . . . splat! They dropped all 98 pounds of me from three feet onto the hard floor. After an unknown time of unconsciousness, I woke up with all the nurses hovering over my bed. I never told my family what happened. I did not want my mom to be troubled with one more piece of bad news.

The day after the frightening, floor-spattering fiasco the doctor in charge of my case appeared at his usual time for morning rounds.

"I'm going to give it to you straight," he said. "The nerve tests on your legs are conclusive. Below your knees to the front to your toes are unresponsive. They are . . . um . . . dead . . . and won't come back to life. You may walk some with leg braces and crutches, but not much. I am so sorry, son."

Grasping the bed rail with my left hand, I lurched up so that I could look at the doctor eye to eye.

"I'm gonna walk out of this hospital. I am!"

He bowed his head, turned and walked away. A strange peace settled over me, and I thought, *I will walk out of here.*

From where did that brave burst of confident zeal come? Supernatural courage rose up within me to defy the giant of permanent nerve damage that was breathing threats against my life and future. This was the beginning of a journey of recovery, hope and power that I believe are convincing proofs of the true God of creation. The lessons I learned along the way have been invaluable in shaping the person that I am today, and they are the foundational principles by which I live my life.

Kind people have paid me lofty compliments, acknowledging my courage, boldness and confidence. Their words are humbling and edifying, yet I must confess that I did not feel worthy of them. The character traits that they mentioned were not traits I had possessed previously. Mere bravado and natural persistence had enabled me to do some extremely untried challenges in my former life; however, those were challenges that had been met with mere natural abilities. The hope and courage that I have now are not based on my own abilities, but rather on the unlimited ability of Jesus' power. Knowing Jesus is what gives me hope and courage.

Turning Point

The year 1968 was arguably one of the worst in American history. President Johnson refused to be nominated for reelection. The troubles of the Vietnam War continued to mount with riots and protests erupting on a continual basis. Martin Luther King Jr. was assassinated in April. Two months later, Robert F. Kennedy was shot. RFK would surely have been elected president instead of Richard Nixon. The Chicago Seven riots, race riots and then . . . in August of that year, my airplane crash.

In December, four months after this catastrophic accident, I was still languishing in a hospital bed barely alive. Even though I had experienced the radiance of God's glory in heaven, the recovery was long and uncertain. There were days of disillusionment and waiting as I had received news that my transfer to a rehabilitation hospital was delayed. I had really hoped to go quickly to accelerate my healing—I was bummed.

On December 21, the TV in my hospital room was on when NASA boldly launched the Saturn V rocket with three astronauts aboard the Apollo 8 mission to circumnavigate the moon. The largest TV audience in history watched as the astronauts' space capsule disappeared behind the dark side of the moon. When that happened, there was over forty minutes of radio silence until they would—hopefully—emerge from behind the moon.

On Christmas Eve, I, along with the rest of the world, watched that black-and-white TV set with tension. Would the astronauts crash into the lunar surface? Would they skip off into space to their death because of lack of gravity? No one knew for sure—not even the scientists.

When in fact they did emerge, the first words we heard were "In the beginning God created the heavens and the earth," as the three Apollo astronauts took turns reading from Genesis 1. When they got to about the tenth verse, I burst out crying. These were not tears of sadness or fear, but tears of joy. The NASA mission, which seemed virtually impossible, began as a bold, brave commitment.

On May 25, 1961, President Kennedy had made a faith declaration that the United States would send men to the moon and bring them back before the end of the decade. What was happening to me as I viewed the fulfillment of his declaration was that my spirit and the Spirit of God inside me began rejoicing in hope. Hope that the impossible was taking place—not only on the moon, but inside of me. None of this understanding was in my conscious mind. It came from deep inside my heart. Spiritual courage was energizing me, and as a result, a beacon of hope was created.

In the months and years that followed, courage to hope produced other miraculous results. Let me share two or three of them:

In May 1969, nine months after the accident, I was moved from the original hospital to a rehabilitation hospital, where I endured dozens of surgical producers and extreme physical therapy daily. The damaged nerves in my left leg produced zero response and, true to the first doctor's initial report, I had to wear a leg brace. The muscles in my right leg were beginning to respond, but I still used a wheelchair and crutches to get around. Even though the doctor had said the nerves were never going to come back, I held on to hope that they would recover fully.

On Thursday, May 15, 1969, physical therapy was canceled because I was scheduled for a surgical procedure that day. Half an hour before the techs came to pick me up for surgery, I was sitting on the bed with my legs dangling over the side. For some reason, I felt compelled to speak to my legs.

"Wake up! Start moving!" I demanded out loud.

Bam! Instantly, both legs came to life and felt completely normal. You need to know that I had no spiritual training in healing, nor had I ever heard of speaking to body parts. I did, however, have this unrealistic optimism—an unexplainable hope. Two months later, in July 1969, I jumped out of an airplane from 12,500 feet and landed safely on those legs. How can this be?

My right hand had been burned so badly that it was not of much use. In October of 1969, a radical operation was performed to attempt to restore some degree of function. This procedure was called an acute deep hand burn covered by a pocket flap-graft. All the scar tissue was peeled off surgically, then my hand—nothing but a mass of raw tissue—was sewn underneath the skin above my rib cage to give my blood a chance to circulate through what was left of my damaged hand. My damaged hand protruded from underneath the skin flap, which was stitched across my wrist. Looking like Napoleon, I had to remain in that position for six weeks. When surgically removed, my hand looked like it had on a tiny boxing glove.

Three months later, a creative and delicate procedure was done to separate the amputed finger bones and create some form of a miniature grasping hand. Three days postoperative, the assistant surgeon came to change the bandage. As the last layer of gauze was unwound, a foul odor emerged.

The doctor said, "Oh no! I'm so sorry, Mr. Robinson. Looks as if we've lost this one." All of the tissue around the stitches was black and smelled like a dead animal.

He bandaged it all up and said sorrowfully, "We'll have to remove it tomorrow."

When the doctor left, I glanced out my hospital window. Golden rays of light shimmered through the glass as the sun was setting over Lake Erie. In that serene moment an idea rose up from within me, and I pressed the call light for the nurse.

When she arrived, I asked, "Please bring me about seven pillows and a floodlight." Without questioning me, she helped me stack up the pillows and placed my bandaged right arm on top of it with the light shining on the bandage.

Silently, I began to command blood to flow from my arm into the dead tissue in my hand. This went on almost all night. My scientific brain should have known the coagulated blood would be like dried Elmer's glue. But the next morning when the doctor came in to set up a surgical field on my bed and began to remove the bandages, he could not believe his eyes.

"Oh my gosh! What?!" he gasped, collapsing against the wall in complete shock.

The previously all-black tissue was now as pink and perfect as a newborn baby's bottom. It was another miracle. My hopes were fulfilled.

My right eye had been blind for five and a half years. I had a cornea from a cadaver attached to my eye three months after my accident. While having these multiple reconstructive surgeries, I was examined occasionally by a world-famous eye surgeon. Barbara and I had begun our life together and were living on our farm in Ashland, Ohio, when I received a phone call from this eye surgeon.

His phone call was a surprise, because for the past year while making periodic visits to the Cleveland University Hospital where he practiced, I would stop this doctor in the hall and say, "If you operate on me, I'll be able to see."

Each time he would kindly, but resolutely, tell me, "Sorry, but you know that is impossible."

This time, however, it was a different story.

"You talked me into it," he said. "Come immediately. We have to finish the operation in less than 24 hours. I have fresh tissue, and this is a live transplant."

Barbara and I raced to Cleveland, which was about an hour and a half away. We checked in to the hospital, and I was on the operating table the next morning. Sandbags lined my head, neck and shoulders, making me completely immobile as I had to remain awake during the delicate two-and-a-half-hour surgery.

When I was returned to my room after the operation, I asked Barbara to have the nursing staff block all light from the windows with black plastic.

I stayed like that for seven days, water-only fasting, and saying over and over, "I can see, I can see, I can see."

What I did not know was that during the operation, my doctor had said to the attending physician, "His eye is completely dead." The iris was wrinkled and stiff, and the pupil was not light reactive. But if the graft worked, I would have some natural color back; the eye would look better cosmetically. At least that was their hope. I, of course, hoped for far more. Seven days later, with Barbara seated beside me in the doctor's office, we unveiled the eye.

"Doc, I can see! I really can see!" I exclaimed as the last piece of gauze was unwound.

He nodded. "Dark shadows? Some light?"

"No, I see both of you! I see you . . . and I see my wife!"

Astonished, he tested me again even more thoroughly and shook his head.

"I can only conclude that this is a miracle!"

My legs were lame, but I hoped to walk. My hand was withered, but I hoped to be able to grasp. I was blind in my right eye for five and a half years, but I hoped to see. The Holy Spirit gave me courage to hope and spiritual bravery for these things and many others, even though I was untrained spiritually. Jesus is the same yesterday, today and forever!

Finding the Courage to Hope

Scripture verses such as Deuteronomy 14:2, Deuteronomy 26:18 and 1 Peter 2:9 tell us that we are God's special treasures—distinct from all others on the face of the earth. We are different not because we sport bumper stickers on our cars or spout Christianese slogans. We are different because our Bible teaches that we are to react with supernatural impulses and not with natural ones. We need supernatural courage to walk with the Lord every day.

Proverbs tells us to "trust in the LORD with all your heart, and lean not on your own understanding; in all your ways acknowledge Him, and He shall direct your paths" (Proverbs 3:5–6). If we are to follow this teaching literally—and since it is God's Word, we are—then *all our ways* means everything and every day. As we walk courageously in the Spirit, we condition ourselves to walk in His ways and in His image as new creatures in Christ.

Spiritual courage affects our will to do His will as He directs our paths. Our daily lives call on us to make choices all of the time. Our internalized values and commitment to the things of the Lord should determine our decisions. As we live and mature there is real value in developing chronic obedience that has the potential to become joyful but still requires courage.

You need supernatural courage to live in an increasingly challenging world—not just to survive a near-death experience. To face challenges that arise in things like marriage and family, you will be required to exercise some of the most Christlike, courageous commitments. It will take costly love and all the fruit and power of the Spirit.

As a pastor and counselor, I have seen many couples fail or fall short. I have also seen terminally ill families not only survive but thrive. It takes guts, commitment, vision and courageous faith to expect God's ways to yield good fruit.

Bringing up children—whether they are spiritual or biological children—will either bring out the best or cause the worst in family dynamics. There is no easy way to train children in the Lord's ways, and families must resolve bravely not to give in or to take frustration out on one another. I have learned that my human strength is limited compared to what the Lord can do. When spiritual courage is exercised and hopeful expectation starts operating, I have a sense of comfort, a feeling of being shielded and the assurance that God is in control. Human effort alone cannot achieve this kind of outcome.

Spiritual bravery is activated as our will aligns with God's will for His purposes. Sometimes the gifts of the Spirit combine, and we are empowered for a specific action. Judges 6:34 says, "The Spirit of the LORD came upon Gideon" (NASB). Another translation renders this verse as follows: "The Spirit of the LORD clothed Gideon" (ESV). Gideon had conquered his own fear of man, defying the wishes of his family and friends by tearing down their idols in the community square. Now he was about to sign up for an insanely hopeless endeavor. He was to take three hundred men and defeat an army that the Bible described as "locusts in abundance, and their camels were without number, as the sand that is on the seashore" (Judges 7:12 ESV). The Holy Spirit clothed Gideon with Himself, and Gideon won the battle.

God wants to use ordinary you in extraordinary ways. The Bible tells us that Christ is in us, and He is the hope of glory (see Colossians 1:27). When life comes at you with high drama or with a mundane annoyance, the Holy Spirit wants to rise up within you. The enemy wants to grind you down, frustrate you, disappoint you and make you feel hopeless and depressed. Jesus is courageous for you. He is why you can have hope. "The eyes of your understanding being enlightened; that you may know what is the hope of His calling, what are the riches of the glory of His inheritance in the saints" (Ephesians 1:18).

How God Defines Hope

Let's explore the word *hope* by God's definition:

Hope is waiting on the Lord—To wait on the Lord is one of the most foundational truths of every believer. "Therefore I will look to the LORD; I will wait for the God of my salvation; my God will hear me" (Micah 7:7).

The Hebrew word used here, *yachal*, means "to wait, to tarry, hope, trust, expect; being patient and to remain in anticipation" (Strong's Concordance). To wait is to expect with hopefulness for God's mercy, His salvation and His rescue. While waiting we are not to take matters into our own hands.

Our hope is based on God's character, His promises, His track record in biblical history and our own experiences. "Wait on the

Lord; be of good courage, and He shall strengthen your heart; wait, I say, on the Lord!" (Psalm 27:14).

Hope is redemptive expectation—One group of people who were hoping for the appearance of the promised Messiah asked John the Baptist if *he* was the One. They were waiting in expectation (see Luke 3:15).

We are learning to keep looking with high hopes until we can see what God is going to do. We are learning that God's promises are worthy of our hope of His coming through for us. We believe that when the Lord fulfills His promises, the result is often much better—even if different—than expected.

Hope is focusing on the prize—The book of First Peter is a letter of hope that was directed especially to the dispersed Jews who were driven to various regions of the world. His letter speaks to our generation, too. "Therefore gird up the loins of your mind, be sober, and rest your hope fully upon the grace that is to be brought to you at the revelation of Jesus Christ" (1 Peter 1:13).

Hope is living—Our hope is not ethereal or philosophical, but real and alive. "Abundant mercy has begotten us again to a *living hope* through the resurrection of Jesus Christ from the dead" (1 Peter 1:3, emphasis added).

Hope is faith in the resurrection power—Peter's sermon at Pentecost (see Acts 2:14–38) includes Psalm 16:8–11. By revelation, Peter is saying that this prophetic psalm is not about David, but rather Jesus the Messiah who conquered death for all who believe in Him. The greatest of all hope is for eternal life. No other religion or spiritual belief makes such an offer.

"Therefore my heart rejoiced, and my tongue was glad; moreover my flesh also will rest in hope. For You will not leave my soul in Hades, nor will You allow Your Holy One to see corruption"

(Acts 2:26–27). The message that Peter preached that day brought in a harvest of 3,000 new believers.

Hope never disappoints—God's Word is clear. It tells us that "we have access by faith into this grace in which we stand, and rejoice in hope of the glory of God. . . . Now *hope does not disappoint*, because the love of God has been poured out in our hearts by the Holy Spirit who was given to us" (Romans 5:2, 5, emphasis added).

Be of good courage and hope expectantly. The Holy Spirit within you will bear witness with your spirit of your redemptive future. Through each chapter in this book, my intention is to express clearly why supernatural courage is essential for everyday life in today's world. I believe and truly hope that the Lord God will impart special grace to you along with activation keys and tools to open the way to your own spiritual adventures.

MEDITATION: Bible Promises for Courage to Hope

Let us hold fast the confession of our hope without wavering, for He who promised is faithful.

Hebrews 10:23

That the God of our Lord Jesus Christ, the Father of glory, may give to you the spirit of wisdom and revelation and the knowledge of Him [to continually know Him better], the eyes of your understanding being enlightened; that you may know what is the hope of His calling.

Ephesians 1:17–18

And we know that all things work together for good to those who love God, to those who are the called according to His purpose.

Romans 8:28

For further reading: Hosea 2:14–15; Colossians 1:27; 1 Thessalonians 4:16–18; 1 Corinthians 13:6–8.

PRAYER for Courage to Hope

Father, you are the God of all hope. I believe the words of Jeremiah: "For I know the thoughts that I think toward you, says the Lord, thoughts of peace and not of evil, to give you a future and a hope" (Jeremiah 29:11). Empower me beyond my natural ability and the boundaries of familiarity. My desire is to be as bold as a lion and to bring You honor. With You, nothing shall be impossible. Baptize me with Your bold love that never fails. In Jesus' name, Amen.

ACTIVATION

- Ponder a time when you prayed and hoped for change in someone who was close to you.
- Remember a season when there was a release of breakthrough and something better than you expected was fulfilled.

DECLARATION

Jesus, I place my hope in You and You alone.

COURAGE TO FOLLOW JESUS

God loves to take the very little we have and give us supernatural
courage to receive the exponential amount He has already provided through our covenant with Him. We only follow Him.

"Papa Joe" Bradford

Would you believe that following Jesus daily takes more courage
than initially choosing to place our faith in Him? We cannot coast
forever on an epic conversion—not even one as mind-blowing as
mine. Not all experiences are the same, of course, but my introduction to the Lord was unique in that it did not take place in a
church setting or with other people.

After the plane crash, the overwhelming manifest presence
of God in that third heaven encounter was gloriously dramatic,
seemingly timeless and with sensations that are still hard to describe. When I woke up, I was full of the Holy Spirit and the
power of God's love, yet I was also in a devastated body that was
fully expected to die. What followed was a series of dramatic
transitions—prophetic communication with the Lord, miracles,

healings and freedom for which I had no theological knowledge or experiential grid.

Apparently, the latter was not necessary at the time. All I had to offer Him was my brokenness and desperation. I did not earn Jesus through my own accomplishments, as daring and brave as I thought they had been. I now knew I could not follow Him in my own strength. No, this was a full surrender and the beginning of an ongoing transformation.

Being conformed to His image is not anything like turning over a new leaf or making a New Year's resolution. One of the best lost-and-found word pictures in the Bible is that of the Prodigal Son. When the son comes to his senses in the pigpen of the far country, he rehearses mentally what he is going to say to his father. In repentance and humility, he decides that he will confess, "Father, I have sinned against heaven and before you, and I am no longer worthy to be called your son. Make me like one of your hired servants" (Luke 15:18–19). That confession took courage.

God will use our weakness to highlight His power. Jesus has provided numerous examples in the Bible and throughout history of people who were empowered by the Holy Spirit and who accomplished extraordinary things far beyond their abilities. The Word of God says in 1 Corinthians 1:27 that "God has chosen the foolish things of the world to put to shame the wise, and God has chosen the weak things of the world to put to shame the things which are mighty." The term *foolish things* points to people who are unqualified in man's eyes to accomplish something their peers would be able to do. *Weak things* applies to people who do not have the power to measure up to the task without the intervention of the Holy Spirit.

"He Gave Me Strength"

May I introduce you to another person who against all odds exercised courage to be a follower of Jesus? The following testimony comes from my friend Joe Bradford.

I was formerly a strong and robust man full of energy, working daily, running a small business and training children in music and the things of God alongside my wife. Suddenly, a rare disease destroyed function in both my kidneys. After months of surgeries and dialysis, I received a kidney transplant requiring the use of immunosuppressive drugs. Doctors told me the heartbreaking news that my life of serving kids was over due to my high susceptibility of contracting diseases, and the fact that the medications I needed to take would cause frequent physical weakness. I no longer could work daily on my small business or be around groups of children.

Nevertheless, Jesus had called me to be a national child advocate for at-risk children and families. My family was led to move into a large, impoverished inner-city community. At that time, God placed His supernatural protection around me to offset the tendency to contract sicknesses from groups of children. Within a few years, God used my weakness and lack of abilities to accent Himself, working through my wife and me to form a charitable and educational program that would affect entire communities. He then used a movie producer to memorialize our story in a movie production that serves as a catalyst to aid underprivileged children in 121 countries.

God loves to take the very little we have and give us supernatural courage to receive the exponential amount He has already provided through our covenant with Him. We only follow Him. Remember that all the heroes of faith in the Bible had natural disadvantages and shortcomings. If Jesus is calling you into a ministry or service beyond your capacity to achieve it, then rejoice! You are primed to receive supernatural courage to move mountains.

I have known Joe Bradford for nearly nineteen years. During this time I have witnessed his spiritual bravery in following the voice of the Lord into uncharted waters at great personal risk. His programs include feeding families in government housing projects in one of the nation's neediest and most dangerous neighborhoods. In this year alone, his organization distributed almost ten thousand Christmas gifts to families who had nothing to give their children, all the while being a light for the Gospel of the Kingdom and a witness for Jesus. Papa Joe is an inspiring speaker who is gifted to motivate others to find their unique God-given callings. He has the courage to follow Jesus. His testimony and the people who have been blessed through his life of service are evidence.

Joe has learned how to walk with Jesus, and he always asks "What's next, Lord?"

As You Received Christ, So Walk in Him

Just as receiving Jesus as Lord involves surrender and ongoing total trust, so does following Him. As it was not in our own strength that we were able to come into relationship with Jesus and His saving grace, we are unable to walk in His ways without His supernatural enabling. But be warned: The courage it takes to be a true follower of Jesus will conflict with our natural or carnal nature "because the carnal mind is enmity [hostile] against God; for it is not subject to the law of God, nor indeed can be" (Romans 8:7). For practical purposes, let's call it human nature.

Radical conversion should begin a process of radical transformation into Christlikeness—not by our own strength, but by the powerful love of God. We are living from the inside out with a brand-new heart and a renewed mind. We are a new creation, people of a new race. Life in this world is very different for us now because we are living in a realm that comes from out of this world, on earth as it is in heaven. "As you therefore have received Christ Jesus the Lord, *so walk in Him*, rooted and built up in Him and established in the faith, as you have been taught, abounding in it with thanksgiving" (Colossians 2:6–7, emphasis added).

In Ephesians, one of the apostle Paul's prison epistles, he writes that we are seated with Him in heavenly places. We no longer walk as we used to walk. We are exhorted how to stand and how to withstand the onslaught of the enemy. We can condense Paul's exhortation in Ephesians to three words: sit, walk and stand.

We live in a world that is in conflict with us as children of God. In our human natures, we might be inclined to run straight into the conflict, tackle it and wrestle with it. In reality, we are to learn how to rest and trust in God's presence. From that presence, we are to learn how to walk supernaturally as the Holy Spirit leads. Then we can withstand the fiery darts of the enemy. Therefore, we can condense Paul's whole exhortation in Ephesians to that simple directive to sit, walk, stand! "For we do not wrestle against flesh and blood, but against principalities, against powers, against the rulers of the darkness of this age, against spiritual hosts of wickedness in the heavenly places" (Ephesians 6:12). God's ways often seem the exact opposite of human nature. Instead of our reacting by charging in and getting entangled in a fight, He often cautions us to pause, rest and respond as we are led by the Spirit.

Biblical Bravehearts

When we talk about the courage needed to walk with the Lord, we only need to look to the Bible to find amazing examples. Let us look at those courageous souls who dared to follow Him in a counterculture much like what exists in today's world, where in some regions it is dangerous to acknowledge Jesus Christ as the Son of God.

In the apostle John's gospel message, we see John the Baptist, the flaming believer like some first-century hippie, wearing an outfit of camel's hair and eating grasshoppers dipped in wild honey. He was right when he identified Jesus as the Lamb of God (see John 1:29). Note that in his declaration, John has confirmation of the prophetic revelation he had received during his time in the wilderness. "I saw the Spirit descending from heaven like a dove, and He remained upon Him. . . . 'This is He who baptizes with the Holy Spirit.' And I have seen and testified that this is the Son of God" (John 1:32–34). The message and the ministry of John the Baptist was radical. The Bible further says, "The people were in expectation, and all reasoned in their hearts about John, whether he was the Christ or not" (Luke 3:15).

Jesus later calls His first disciples from among those who had followed John. We must assume it took plenty of courage to identify with that wild man in the midst of the current religious and political climate. His prophetic ministry stirred up the messianic hopes of both the general population and the religious elites who would later plot to crucify Jesus.

Andrew is named as one of the first two disciples; the other was probably John, the author of this gospel. The first four disciples left their nets (their secular fishing businesses) to follow Jesus. Beyond that fact, there is not much detail of what it was like or who took care of their families—although Peter once declared passionately, "See, we have left all and followed You" (Matthew 19:27).

Modern-Day Bravehearts

I want to mention a couple of modern-day Jesus followers who chose the courage of their convictions to change their careers and destinies.

Keith Thibodeaux was the child actor who played Little Ricky on the *I Love Lucy* TV show. He also had the role of one of Opie's best friends on *The Andy Griffith Show*. A child prodigy as a drummer, Keith played drums in a very successful rock band after his TV career. When Keith found Jesus as his personal Savior, his band, David and the Giants, also converted to a "Jesus freak" band. Today Keith and his wife, Kathy, lead the premier Christian ballet company Ballet Magnificat!. With great artistic excellence, they glorify Jesus all over the world. Most likely Keith could have been a movie star. Instead, he chose to point people to the Bright and Morning Star (see Revelation 22:16).

Another amazing artist who showed great courage is guitarist Phil Keaggy. His band, Glass Harp, won a battle of the bands contest and was awarded a recording contract. After three premier record albums, Phil was recognized as one of the greatest guitar players on the modern music scene at a time when names like Clapton, Hendrix and Joe Walsh were electrifying large crowds. Phil often played his soaring solos in front of the same type of large crowds.

Phil Keaggy had a dramatic encounter with Jesus about the time of his first recording. Afterward, he testified humbly but boldly about Jesus at his concerts, soon commanding the respect of even the music moguls. On one occasion, he was playing outside before a crowd of a hundred thousand people under black storm clouds along Lake Erie. By the time his band completed their set, the clouds had parted and the sun was shining. The MC, who was the most well-known disc jockey in America, was overheard saying that there must really be something about this Jesus stuff. Today Phil's guitar prowess is more incredible than ever, and he continues to have an impact on the lives of multitudes.

I know this is true because these tenderhearted men and their families have been my friends for decades. What an honor. I have seen their genuine faith and values up close and personal as they exalt the name that is above all names, Jesus their Lord.

Counting the Cost

I have heard it said that salvation is a free gift from God, but discipleship will cost you everything. Unlike Keith and Phil, some people decide that the cost is too high. Such was the case of the rich young ruler of Mark 10. His story goes like this:

After encountering Jesus one day, a young man asks, "Good Teacher, what good thing shall I do that I may have eternal life?"

"If you want to enter into eternal life, keep the commandments," Jesus replies.

"Which ones?" the young man wants to know.

"You already know them: Do not commit adultery. Do not murder. Do not steal. Do not bear false witness. Honor your father and mother. Do not covet what belongs to your neighbor."

"Well, I've kept all these things since I was a kid," the young man insists. Then Jesus looks him right in the eye.

And looking at him, Jesus *loved* him. (I wonder if in that moment the Lord was thinking, *This young guy is about My age. I know how he's feeling. It's hard for him to relinquish all that he has acquired—the material things that he believes make him happy.*)

In His compassion, Jesus must have hesitated a moment longer before adding, "One thing you lack: Go your way, sell whatever you have and give it to the poor. Then you will have treasure in heaven."

It is then that He issues the royal invitation, the most valuable gift the young man would ever receive—far greater than his worldly riches.

"Come, take up the cross and follow Me."

But when the young man hears the conditions imposed by that invitation, he turns it down and leaves filled with sorrow.

This part of Scripture has always bothered me a little. Perhaps it is a safeguard for me not to become too casual or too familiar about following Jesus. However, I do not believe that this stipulation regarding finances or possessions applies to everyone. I believe it was specific to this young man.

I doubt that the rich young ruler really understood how much he was loved that day. If he had, he would have gladly accepted Jesus' invitation. The key to having the courage to follow Christ is experiencing the incomparable love of God.

Paul, a former religious zealot, counted all of his pedigree and experience as loss. His résumé was impeccable. He was

> circumcised the eighth day, of the stock of Israel, of the tribe of Benjamin, a Hebrew of the Hebrews; concerning the law, a Pharisee; concerning zeal, persecuting the church; concerning the righteousness which is in the law, blameless.
>
> Philippians 3:5–6

Despite his credentials, he counted it all "rubbish, that I may gain Christ and be found in Him, not having my own righteousness, which is from the law, but that which is through faith in Christ" (verses 8–9). It is probable that Paul had a fairly noble birth, as he stated that he was a Roman citizen (see Acts 22:28). It is apparent that Paul found Jesus more wonderful and fascinating than any title, wealth or status because he had experienced the love and forgiveness that set him free.

Other prominent biblical characters also did not count the cost too high to lay down their own agendas or, in some cases, their reputations and their lives:

Mary, the mother of Jesus—Hearing the announcement from the angel Gabriel that she would conceive a child after being overshadowed by the Holy Spirit, she hesitated only momentarily and then said, "Let it be to me according to your word" (Luke 1:38). This is the ultimate example of courage under unprecedented circumstances. What would the town gossips say?

Joseph, her fiancé—While trying to find a compassionate way out of a delicate predicament, Joseph had a dream. God's angel spoke to him in the dream:

> "Joseph, son of David, don't hesitate to get married. Mary's pregnancy is Spirit-conceived. God's Holy Spirit has made her pregnant. She will bring a son to birth, and when she does, you, Joseph, will name him Jesus—'God saves'—because he will save his people from their sins."
>
> Matthew 1:20–21 MSG

Ananias—This disciple from Damascus heard the Lord in a vision instruct him to go to a certain street in town and ask for a man named Saul of Tarsus, a known persecutor of Christians. Ananias was to lay hands on him so his blinded eyes could see. It is no surprise that Ananias would question this strange directive:

"Master, you can't be serious. Everybody's talking about this man and the terrible things he's been doing, his reign of terror against your people in Jerusalem! And now he's shown up here with papers from the Chief Priest that give him license to do the same to us." But the Master said, "Don't argue. Go! I have picked him as my personal representative to non-Jews and kings and Jews. And now I'm about to show him what he's in for—the hard suffering that goes with this job."

Acts 9:13–16 MSG

In obedience, yet likely fearing for his life, Ananias found the house, placed his hands on the blind man and said, "Brother Saul, the Master sent me, the same Jesus you saw on your way here. He sent me so you could see again and be filled with the Holy Spirit" (verses 17–18 MSG).

Talk about hard-core trust and obedience by this supernaturally brave follower of Jesus. Ananias even called the former bad guy "brother," acknowledging that he believed in Saul's true conversion.

The courage it took these precious people to believe the leading of the Lord and to follow through with their actions is a powerful testimony that it can be done. In these examples, we can see that spiritual bravery is based on relationship. Courage and obedience are not about accomplishment, but rather building relationships. "For as many as are led by the Spirit of God, these are sons of God. For you did not receive the spirit of bondage again to fear, but you received the Spirit of adoption by whom we cry out, 'Abba, Father'" (Romans 8:14–15).

The Jesus Revolution

This phenomenal move of the Holy Spirit sprang up and then exploded worldwide in the last part of the 20th century. The

Jesus-movement radicals surrendered many or all of their ideologies/beliefs—things like world peace, seeking the "truth," anti-establishment movements, sexual revolutionary concepts, recreational drugs, occult spiritual beliefs and many other mixtures of influence. As followers of Jesus, they learned that peace and truth are found in a person. These passionate new followers of the Lord Jesus learned and experienced that there is only one way. They found the way in the person of Jesus Christ the Messiah.

Most of these new zealots referred to themselves simply as Jesus People. Non-Christian hippies dubbed them Jesus Freaks, much like the nonbelievers in the city of Antioch called the radical believers *Christians*, meaning "little Christs." In those days, this label was more pejorative than a compliment. Churches that experienced Jesus Freaks merging into their established congregations had to adjust their theology. Even with their long hair, tie-dyed T-shirts, holes in their jeans, miniskirts and sometimes even bare feet, these passionate new believers were welcomed.

They emphasized a personal relationship with Jesus and not merely church attendance. It was Jesus every day. These strong new believers practiced their faith openly and unashamedly, unafraid to promote healing, Bible study, prayer and sincere praise and worship every day, not just on Sunday.

Their contributions to existing churches transformed meetings from traditional with a stiff formality to warm and enthusiastic. Services now reflected a renewal of the heart and mind, incorporating musical instruments—guitars, electronic keyboards, drums, flutes, tambourines, etc. This happened with the approval of leadership because of the powerful fruit that accompanied this restoration. There was no shyness, no timidity as they boldly proclaimed their faith, whether one-on-one or to a crowd. They even took their instruments to park gatherings and were able to lead many to Jesus.

God was real. Compelled by a burning love, His newest children wanted to share Him. If you were there, you know what I am talking about. As I write, the overpowering presence of the Holy

Spirit is so strong that I need to pull away from the computer to spend time worshiping my Lord . . . *Selah.*

As you follow the path the Lord lays before you, be of good courage. On this course, there will be provision and protection as He displays His strength through you. Keep your eyes on Jesus, the author and finisher of your faith. He is praying for you to follow Him. "Father, I desire that they also whom You gave Me may be with Me where I am" (John 17:24).

MEDITATION: Bible Promises for Courage to Follow Jesus

And everyone who has left houses or brothers or sisters or father or mother or wife or children or lands, for My name's sake, shall receive a hundredfold, and inherit eternal life.

Matthew 19:29

Trust in the LORD with all your heart, and lean not on your own understanding; in all your ways acknowledge Him, and He shall direct your paths.

Proverbs 3:5–6

I am the way, the truth, and the life. No one comes to the Father except through Me.

John 14:6

For further reading: Colossians 1:13; John 8:31–32.

PRAYER for Courage to Follow Jesus

Lord, I thank You that You always hear my voice. I ask that I would be able to hear Your voice continually. As You speak,

*grant me the boldness to follow through with what You are
asking me to do. Let me walk in Your ways and find favor
and strength that empowers me to serve You. Let Your Word
resound in me, for Your Word is a lamp for my feet. Lord, I
ask that You would lead me to the path that is higher than
I. In Jesus' name, Amen.*

ACTIVATION

- Ask God each day to help you reach someone for Him. Do
  not hesitate to ask others, "Are you a follower of Jesus?"
  You will experience the Holy Spirit giving you non-
  offensive ways to share the love of God.
- Pray for people if they mention their need of healing or
  freedom from some habitual sin or weakness. Even if they
  refuse your offer of prayer, you will leave them with a
  memory of authentic kindness.

DECLARATION

I am a follower of King Jesus, not a prisoner of intimidation. I
will proclaim my faith boldly!

COURAGE TO BE HUMBLE

We may impress people with our strengths,
but we connect with people through our vulnerabilities.

Nicky Gumbel, Vicar, Holy Trinity Church,
London, England

People who feel so strong in the natural that they do not need any help, any reinforcements or the strength of God's love are on their own. "A man who isolates himself seeks his own desire; he rages against all wise judgment" (Proverbs 18:1). Godly followers of the Lord who have the honesty to admit their own weaknesses run in humility to Him. Lifestyle humility is the foundation for enduring strength and for performing supernatural acts that bring glory to God without the strings of self-recognition or selfish ambition.

Let me begin with a confession/vision from my own unenlightened past:

Was I dreaming . . . or was I standing on the porch of our farmhouse that we had just acquired staring at a surreal scene across the road? A big tour bus had veered off into a ditch and was stuck hubcap-deep in thick mud. Instantly, I was transported closer to the huge vehicle and could see the faces of trapped passengers who were mouthing cries of distress. Although I could not hear a sound, I could still sense their anxiety and desperate desire to be free.

Glancing toward the front of the bus I saw a well-dressed man in a three-piece suit. I recognized him as the host of a popular Christian television show. As a frequent viewer of his program, I knew that he was articulate and experienced in ministering to multitudes by the power of God. Yet he was not doing a thing about their plight. He just kept looking in my direction.

There I stood in my farm gear—overalls, flannel shirt and work boots. Yes, I was young and enthusiastic about Jesus, but I was inexperienced in ministry.

When this well-known leader continued to make no move to help the people, I lifted one hand toward them and said, "In Jesus' . . ." Before I could utter the word *name* the doors and windows popped open and the grateful passengers spilled out, delighted to be free.

I was shocked and stunned at how easy that deliverance had been.

"Wow! That was eas—" But before I could finish my thought, I was in the driver's seat of a tow truck racing in reverse at lightning speed. Afraid that I was going to crash into something, I rammed my left foot on the brake pedal. I was just about to shout "Jesus!" when I woke up in bed, my left foot jammed against the footboard.

It was then I heard the voice of the Lord speaking to me.

When you start moving in power and setting people free, do not take yourself seriously. You could end up going backward.

This was to be a major life lesson for me. As much as it took courage to humble myself and trust God to provide for my wife and me as we began the work of ministry, it would require an even greater kind of spiritual bravery not to claim the glory that belongs to God when we see His power moving through us.

Lifestyle Humility

To give you a better idea of the process through which the Lord has brought me, here is a little of the backstory of the dream that was a major defining moment in my life. Years ago, Barbara and I were able to buy an old farmhouse on fourteen acres of lush farmland. The house came with a detached garage and a magnificent barn, complete with a "Chew Mail Pouch Tobacco" ad painted on the side. This move was an uncalculated, whimsical attempt at self-sufficiency by two young, big city suburbanites with zero training. What were we thinking?

Not long after our move we recognized our lack of farmyard skills, and I began to work some regular jobs. We lived outside of a quaint Midwestern college town where working-class people made up the majority of the population.

A few weeks after our first child, Michael, was born, God called us into full-time ministry. We were to live by faith—no regular paycheck—just trusting God to provide. As the doors began to open for me to share my testimony, to teach and to preach the message of Jesus and His Kingdom, I experienced real joy in this gutsy adventure.

I must admit it took a lot of unnatural bravery to quit my job when I had the real responsibilities of a home, wife and child. All of that required money. It was Barbara who encouraged me to go this route, telling me how God was confirming to her that we were to live by faith. From Scripture, I knew that supporting my family was my responsibility. God gave me that extraordinary dream and a lesson in humility that I remembered for the rest of my life. To echo Paul's words,

> For I am the least of the apostles, who am not worthy to be called an apostle, because I persecuted the church of God. But by the grace of God I am what I am, and His grace toward me was not in vain; but I labored more abundantly than they all [other apostles], yet not I, but the grace of God which was with me.
>
> 1 Corinthians 15:9–10

Let's make a note that a lifestyle of humility is one of the foundational ways of God. It is not about self-abasement. In the passage above, Paul acknowledges his grievous sin in persecuting the Church, while at the same time recognizing the quantity and quality of his ministry that was accomplished by God's grace.

A modern-day church father, Francis Frangipane, coined the phrase "Humility is the stronghold of the godly."[1] This is born for us in our supernatural, new creation nature, not from our natural human nature. Pride is so natural to fallen man that it springs up in his heart like weeds in a watered garden. No one has more pride than someone who is deceived into believing that he or she is not prideful.

"Therefore humble yourselves under the mighty hand of God, that He may exalt you in due time" (1 Peter 5:6). It is our job to humble ourselves; it is God's job to exalt us. If we start doing His job (exalting ourselves), He will start doing our job (humbling us). And I tell you quite passionately, you do not want God doing your job. He is always an overachiever!

Humility Leads to Repentance

If the repentant ones who have lost their way turn to the Lord, He will surely guide them in His ways. "Good and upright is the LORD; therefore He teaches sinners in the way. The *humble He guides* in justice, and the *humble He teaches* His way" (Psalm 25:8–9, emphasis added).

While correction in the moment may feel like punishment, it is really liberating love from our true Father. I shared in the first chapter how I had emerged from my brush with death to find that not only had I changed, but the world had also changed. The late '60s and early '70s were the age of Woodstock, the hippie movement and free love. That mixture proved to be incompatible with the Lordship of Jesus Christ. Those who mentored and discipled me helped me to choose to walk bravely in humility that led to freedom.

We live in an era when there are many wrong influences in public media. Humility will help us to have clearer sensitivity to His presence that will purify our daily lives. Every move of God brings about confrontational change. This causes those who are brave to yield humbly to the convincing and convicting work of the Holy Spirit. This repentance may come as a result of an awakening to the power of God or to an awareness that the Lord expects His followers to follow the example that He provided for us while He was on earth.

In our awakening, we will often say, "There's got to be more! Lord, I want more. I need more!" Grace covers us, but courageous humility allows us to uncover our need for the power of the Lord, humbly expecting that He will fulfill that need with His unrelenting love and power.

"Two men went up to the temple to pray, one a Pharisee and the other a tax collector. The Pharisee stood and prayed thus with himself, 'God, I thank You that I am not like other men—extortioners, unjust, adulterers, or even as this tax collector. I fast twice a week; I give tithes of all that I possess.' And the tax collector, standing afar off, would not so much as raise his eyes to heaven, but beat his breast, saying, 'God, be merciful to me a sinner!' I tell you, this man went down to his house justified rather than the other; for everyone who exalts himself will be humbled, and he who humbles himself will be exalted."

Luke 18:10–14

Pray to Be Broken

In March of 1983, a small group of men from our church attended a men's conference in Columbus, Ohio. The first night, shortly after worship began, I heard a voice say to me, *Pray to be broken. Where did that come from?* I wondered. *Did I imagine it?*

Five minutes later, I heard the same message again: *Listen, I want you to pray to be broken.*

Now I was beginning to get it. It must be the Lord.

In obedience, I shot up a quick prayer: *Lord, I ask You that I would be broken.* I then joined in the rest of the worship and listened to the excellent speaker. Afterward, the guys and I went up to our hotel rooms, had pop and pizza, joked around a little and then turned in.

The next morning began with a little time of worship, testimonies about what others had experienced from the previous night, preaching and then a lunch break. Not for a moment had I thought about my prayer about being broken.

After lunch, we returned to the meeting room and took our seats. A guest worship leader started singing "Jesus Loves Me"—the little kids song. He then moved into "Oh, How He Loves You and Me." With that, I burst into uncontrollable weeping that was heaving forward from the depths of my gut. I was in travail in a room with five hundred other men. My friend and pastor put his arm around me as the worship and my tears continued. There had been nothing going on in my life that I was aware of—no crisis, no unconfessed sin or relational issue—that would have justified this kind of brokenness. After about twenty minutes I stopped crying, but I could not speak and I could not think. It was like I was in a catatonic state.

I was scheduled to leave the conference a little early as I was a guitar player in a band, and we had an outreach to play at about an hour or so north. One of the band members, the keyboard player and lead singer, had been with me at the conference. As he drove us to the concert site, I sat in the back seat still unable to speak, with my head resting against the car window. I was staring ahead without conscious thought or emotion. The band members who had arrived earlier had already set up the equipment, so as soon as we reached the campground, they led me to where I was supposed to play. As we started our first song, my brain recalibrated suddenly and switched on.

Our ministry time was to consist of our band playing some contemporary Christian rock music, then my sharing my testimony, preaching a message and giving an invitation. There was nothing particularly heavy in my message, and yet as I extended an invitation for total surrender to the Lord, some eighty people of all ages moved forward. They were weeping and heaving just as I had done a few hours earlier. On their knees in travail, they received the Lord for the first time. One sixteen-year-old girl was the last child of a family of twelve to give her heart to the Lord. Her mom and dad were there celebrating their 32nd wedding anniversary, and they were ecstatic over their daughter's decision.

I had never seen or heard anything like this. Somehow, by God's supernatural power, the brokenness the Lord had asked me to experience was imparted to them. Having humility and being willing to yield causes vulnerability. Thankfully, I was open to the Lord. I obeyed Him when He asked me to pray to be broken even though I did not know the reason why. In retrospect, I saw that I had been emptied out completely so that I could be filled to impart God's saving grace to people I had never met.

False Humility Is Stinking Thinking

There is a mistaken sense of humility when people examine themselves and conclude that they are worthless. This kind of thinking discounts or forgets the reality that we are created in the image of God and that we have inherited everything needed for "life and godliness" (2 Peter 1:3).

False humility is just as self-centered as prideful arrogance. It does not see the redemptive hope that is always available to us by the power of the Holy Spirit. This is very deceptive as it carries the semblance of humility, yet denies the goodness of God and the many times He has shown Himself to us.

False humility does not allow us to see our own virtues and gifts. It also hinders our ability to recognize that we have legitimate needs and that God has the available grace and power to provide them. We could miss these as opportunities for increase in His abundance by stinky thinking and declaring lack. Vain imagination is not only relegated to grandiose ideas of the high-minded, but also when a downward spiral of negativity vexes our hearts and minds. These weeds try to rise up quickly to choke out our fruitfulness.

Instead, welcome true humility. Start choosing genuine dependence on the Holy Spirit. Keep looking to the Lord until you can see redemptive solutions and answers that reflect wisdom born from above. He has taken us out of darkness and into the light. The spiritually brave ones trust God in His leading by the Holy Spirit even in unfamiliar areas. Often just inviting the Lord's guidance in prayer and meditation clothes you with humility.

True Humility: Gateway to Revival

A verse that has always been a personal treasure of mine is found in Isaiah:

> For thus says the High and Lofty One who inhabits eternity, whose name is Holy: "I dwell in the high and holy place, with him who has a contrite and humble spirit, to revive the spirit of the humble, and to revive the heart of the contrite ones."
>
> Isaiah 57:15

In other words, we are not to remain frozen in our brokenness; rather, we are to keep seeking the Lord, who is eager to revive us.

Is it not indicative of the character of the Lord that He loved humanity so much that He sent His only begotten Son to give us abundant life (see John 3:16)? It should be obvious that redemption is all about revival. The message of the Good News is not how angry God is, but how good God is in His desire to revive our spirits.

> You have turned for me my mourning into dancing; You have put off my sackcloth and clothed me with gladness, to the end that my

glory may sing praise to You and not be silent. O LORD my God, I will give thanks to You forever.

Psalm 30:11–12

Another of my favorite verses is found in Isaiah. It is part of our Lord's mission statement:

To console those who mourn in Zion, to give them beauty for ashes, the oil of joy for mourning, the garment of praise for the spirit of heaviness; that they may be called trees of righteousness, the planting of the LORD, that He may be glorified.

Isaiah 61:3

Who does not want consolation in their grief? Beauty instead of death and disease? Joy in the midst of suffering? How can we not desire revival? How can we be silent? Shout for joy right now. Wipe your tears and get up and dance!

Jesus, the Perfect Model of Humility

It is an amazing dynamic that the Lord is the gold standard of true humility. Just as amazing is that we are to follow His example.

Have this attitude in yourselves which was also in Christ Jesus, who, although He existed in the form of God, did not regard equality with God a thing to be grasped, but emptied Himself, taking the form of a bond-servant, and being made in the likeness of men. Being found in appearance as a man, He humbled Himself by becoming obedient to the point of death, even death on a cross.

Philippians 2:5–8 NASB

Even near the end of Jesus' earthly life some of the disciples were still jockeying for position. They came to Him and asked, "Who then is greatest in the kingdom of heaven?" (Matthew 18:1). Jesus called a little child over and placed him in the midst of the group. "Unless you are converted and become as little children, you will by no means enter the kingdom of heaven. Therefore whoever humbles himself as this little child is the greatest in the kingdom of heaven" (Matthew 18:3–4). Even in the midst of the ambitious disciples trying to climb the company ladder, they were taught a lesson in humility.

In a move that must have shocked all of them, Jesus taught a supreme lesson in courageous servanthood. On the eve of His betrayal after the Passover supper, He wrapped a towel around His waist and filled a basin with water. Bending low before one after the other, including Judas, Jesus began to wash their dirty feet that were stained from years of walking on the desert sands. Only the lowliest of servants would stoop to fulfill that necessity. I am sure they exchanged looks of sheer disbelief that their Lord and Master, the King of the universe, would serve them in this humble way.

But that was just the point, right?

Coming to Peter, Jesus was met with resistance. He, however, explained, "You do not understand what is going on now, but you will after this" (see John 13:7).

When He finished this menial task, Jesus put his robe back on and sat down.

> "Do you know what I have done to you? You call Me Teacher and Lord, and you say well, for so I am. If I then, your Lord and Teacher, have washed your feet, you also ought to wash one another's feet. For I have given you an example, that you should do as I have done to you. Most assuredly, I say to you, a servant is not greater than his master; nor is he who is sent greater than he who sent him. If you know these things, blessed are you if you do them."
>
> John 13:12–17

This demonstration speaks loudly. Even though Jesus came as a king and conqueror, His actions among His people were those of an extraordinary servant.

Meekness Is Not Weakness

As Jesus was journeying toward Jerusalem, He sent James and John ahead to prepare for His arrival. Unfortunately, the residents of a Samaritan village along the way were not very hospitable and were unwilling to allow Jesus to come. Indignant at this insult to their Lord, James and John asked Jesus,

> "Lord, do You want us to command fire to come down from heaven and consume them, just as Elijah did?"
>
> But He turned and rebuked them, and said, "You do not know what manner of spirit you are of. For the Son of Man did not come to destroy men's lives but to save them." And they went to another village.
>
> Luke 9:54–56

Apparently, the disciples assumed that Elijah had set a spiritual precedent when he executed the prophets of Baal at Mount Carmel (see 1 Kings 18:40).

The Jews and the Samaritans had been enemies for centuries. In spite of their hostility, the Lord's heart was to bless and not to destroy—even though it was within His power to reduce His reluctant hosts to ashes.

Although Jesus describes Himself as lowly and meek, He is still the Lord of all and the supreme commander of the heavenly hosts. He is a mighty warrior. "The LORD is with me like a dread champion" (Jeremiah 20:11 NASB).

Humility is power under control. The courage to be humble is joined by the fruit of the Spirit of self-control. It is a supernatural ability to hold back when you are being provoked, when you are challenged by circumstances or when you are with people who push your buttons.

Take, for example, Jesus in the Garden of Gethsemane when Judas comes to betray Him with a kiss. Accompanying Judas is a massive armed guard. Feisty Peter, in defense of his master, swings his sword and cuts off a guard's ear. Jesus tells him to sheathe his sword, adding, "Don't you know that I could just pray to my Father and He would provide Me with more than twelve legions of angels?" (see Matthew 26:53).

Twelve legions? One Roman legion is six thousand men. If my calculations are right, that would be 72,000 angels. That angelic army could completely rearrange all of the Middle East, liberate and take over every country, and utilize the oil wells to provide power past my 120th birthday. Jesus had unparalleled strength and power at His access, and yet He chose not to use it to defend Himself.

It is liberating when you find joy in walking in humility. There is a freedom in experiencing the sensation that you are living in a noncompete zone. You do not have to play the game. In this digital age of self-promotion through social media, having the courage to be humble can cause you to walk safely through the minefield of grandiose identity. Everybody wants everybody to know who they are and how they shine.

Though there are truly appropriate and inspiring ways for people to express themselves without being self-serving, humble people are usually recognized by others who can perceive that they are really who they appear to be. When we walk in humility by the grace of God, we see things very differently. There is more empathy and compassion and less judgment and rejection. Jesus was approachable by those who had been marked and rejected. He touched and healed the leper. He raised the dead. Touching either of them would have made Him ceremonially unclean according to the Law.

Check out His itinerary to get an idea of the kind of people with whom He mingled:

> Then Jesus went about all the cities and villages, teaching in their synagogues, preaching the gospel of the kingdom, and healing every sickness and every disease among the people. But when He saw the multitudes, He was moved with compassion for them, because they were weary and scattered, like sheep having no shepherd.

Then He said to His disciples, "The harvest truly is plentiful, but the laborers are few. Therefore pray the Lord of the harvest to send out laborers into His harvest."

Matthew 9:35–38

We can be the answer to that prayer. Although the problems in our communities today might seem overwhelming, when we are moved with His compassion we can become courageously humble. When that happens, we will see people as the Lord sees them.

With this brave humility comes the boldness to do something about it. Humility causes us to partner in a greater way with the Holy Spirit. We get to be real colaborers with our Lord. Would you rather attempt to do things on your own or have God do the heavy lifting?

MEDITATION: Bible Promises for Courage to Be Humble

Blessed are the poor in spirit, for theirs is the kingdom of heaven. . . . Blessed are the meek, for they shall inherit the earth.

Matthew 5:3, 5

Whoever exalts himself will be humbled, and he who humbles himself will be exalted.

Matthew 23:12

When pride comes, then comes disgrace, but with the humble is wisdom.

Proverbs 11:2 ESV

You are the people of God; he loved you and chose you for his own. So then, you must clothe yourselves with compassion, kindness, humility, gentleness, and patience.

Colossians 3:12 GNT

For further reading: 2 Samuel 6:22; Proverbs 11:2; Zephaniah 3:11–12; James 4:6; Psalm 139:23–24.

PRAYER for Courage to Be Humble

Lord, grant me the grace to live my life clothed in Your power and authority so that You are the One who is lifted high. Father, as Your child let me be aware that I am accepted in the beloved. That is more than enough personal recognition for me to feel secure. Let me be as the elders in heaven in the book of Revelation who cast their crown before Your throne. Whenever my life has the power of influence toward others, let them recognize that I have been in Your presence. In Jesus' name, Amen.

ACTIVATION

- Recognize occasions where you might have a tendency to bring honor to yourself. Instead, humble yourself and acknowledge God and His goodness in your life.
- Find someone who will agree with you in prayer that God will manifest glorious strength through you through the courage to be humble.

DECLARATION

God exalts me as I humble myself and glorify Him.

COURAGE TO FIGHT

We have always needed God from the very beginning of this nation, but today we need Him especially. We are facing a new kind of enemy. We're involved in a new kind of warfare. And we need the help of the Spirit of God.

Dr. Billy Graham, in an address to the nation after 9/11

I doubt I need to tell you that we are at war with our archenemy, Satan. Those who acknowledge God—followers of Jesus in particular—are in his crosshairs as never before.

If he cannot wipe out God's people one way, he will try another way. He has many tricks up his sleeve. Our faith and exploits in the Lord will be tested, and the enemy will try to defeat us. But we have resources—a powerful arsenal the world neither understands nor knows how to use. How we fight in the Spirit is different from how the rest of the world wages war. It is time we armed up. The following story is about a valiant woman in Atlanta who through years of intercessory prayer was prepared to fight during a school-shooting crisis.

On August 20, 2013, Antoinette Tuff was working as a school bookkeeper alone in the front office of McNair Discovery Learning

Academy in Atlanta. She had a mountain of troubles: a recent divorce (her husband of 33 years left her for another woman), a suicide attempt, a disabled son, and a car that was about to be repossessed.

It was under those circumstances that she heard the words "We are going to all die today!"[1] from a twenty-year-old former student holding both an AK-47 and over five hundred rounds of ammunition. She discerned that the young man was unstable mentally and called 911. The school filled quickly with SWAT team snipers who were hoping to get a clear shot.

Antoinette talked calmly with the shooter and convinced him to lay down his weapon and surrender. During the tense moments of the standoff, Antoinette relied heavily on her relationship with the Lord. She said to an NPR reporter, "I was calling on Him more than I'm calling on Him any day. I was like, 'God, what we going to do now, what we going to do next, what do I say, how do I say it?'"[2]

When asked about her calm demeanor, Antoinette stated, "I was screaming and terrified on the inside. I didn't even know I was calm until everybody kept saying that. And so what I did is I went back to listen to the 911 tape to see exactly what I was saying and how calm I was. And to be honest with you, I didn't even recognize my own voice. And so I knew at that moment that it was God who guided me through that day."[3]

I am sure that the best-case scenario the officials were hoping for was a sniper having a good shot at this young man. Instead, the Holy Spirit was working through this woman's intercession and spiritual bravery. As succinctly tweeted by Kathy Groob, "Antoinette Tuff used kindness and love in the face of terror, saved lives and showed true courage."[4] Supernatural courage saved many, many lives that day.

Perilous Times Will Come

We would be naïve and unprepared not to heed the admonitions that the apostle Paul gives us in his epistles to Timothy. "Now the Spirit expressly says that in latter times some will depart from the faith, giving heed to deceiving spirits and doctrines of demons, speaking lies in hypocrisy, having their own conscience seared with a hot iron" (1 Timothy 4:1–2). Is this not an apt description of the times in which we are now living? Just this week some notable Christian leaders have departed from the faith. Frighteningly prophetic. Brother Paul warned us,

> But know this, that in the last days perilous times will come: For men will be lovers of themselves, lovers of money, boasters, proud, blasphemers, disobedient to parents, unthankful, unholy, unloving, unforgiving, slanderers, without self-control, brutal, despisers of good, traitors, headstrong, haughty, lovers of pleasure rather than lovers of God, having a form of godliness but denying its power. And from such people turn away!
>
> 2 Timothy 3:1–5

Second Timothy was the last letter Paul wrote before his death. He was imprisoned as he wrote it; however, this imprisonment was not like his previous house arrest where people could come to visit him and during which he wrote the notable prison epistles. This time Paul was confined to a dank dungeon. He was elderly, cold, lonely and aware that he may not survive. His last words and testament are extremely important.

In this letter, there are at least seventeen directives, admonitions or commands that Paul uses to exhort Timothy, his beloved son in the faith. He urges him to follow these in order to protect his life and the lives of those in the Church. I mention only one here, but I encourage you to read the entire letter for yourself in order to be prepared.

The first exhortation occurs after a very personal, warm and tender introduction. "I remind you to stir up the gift of God which is in you through the laying on of my hands" (2 Timothy 1:6).

We are called upon to take action—to stir up. To "fan into flame" and "kindle afresh" are other translations of this phrase

(ESV, NASB). To be filled with both the Holy Spirit and the Word of God is how we prepare to courageously fight our adversary. It is something we have to do so that we will stand and not fall, and so that the shield of faith will extinguish the fiery arrows of the enemy (see Ephesians 6:16).

Paul's word is clear—we must be prepared. The next assault may come from a direction we are least expecting. It happened to me.

A Frontal Assault

Two years after my wife and I had begun our lives together, our marriage came under a serious attack. As a result, we separated. We were in grave danger of losing our marriage, and I was seeking the Lord for His help. In raw, desperate bravery, I had been fasting without food or water for three days. At that time, I did not even know the meaning or significance of a total fast. I had been gripped with such anxiety that I could neither eat nor drink. I could only pray.

On this particular day, my mind was being attacked, and I was experiencing dark revelations. I was being led to believe that all our problems were my fault and that there was no hope. So severe was this onslaught of evil accusations that I was paralyzed by fear. I was under siege unlike anything I had yet experienced.

After many hours, the voice of the Holy Spirit moved through me with clarity and authority and spoke these words to my broken heart: *What you did was an act of love.* I knew exactly what the Spirit was saying. Buying that farm was done out of love— providing security for my wife and fulfilling her heart's desire. This message of hope coursing through me came like a spiritual nuclear blast, and it shattered the construct of the enemy's assault.

Simultaneously, four hundred miles away, my wife was filled and endued with power by the Holy Spirit. In that moment, she wrote out a page of declarative prophecy of her life mission without really realizing what she was doing. The next day, I flew to where she was, and we both flew home together. We began living a marriage fully committed to each other. What the enemy intended for evil, God turned for good. I cannot overemphasize how one true phrase from God—eight little words in this case—can demolish the stronghold of the enemy.

Discerning Our True Enemy

One of the most important tools in spiritual warfare is discernment. This is the ability to determine whether or not we are engaged in battle with the enemy. There is a drastic difference between battling demonic forces and battling our own fleshly desires, being tempted by the allure of the world we live in or suffering self-inflicted consequences. In these cases, blame-shifting onto the devil will not bring victory.

Remember, the way we fight spiritual battles is very different from the strategies used in the natural. It is imperative to know who we are and to know experientially who the Lord really is as we seek victory. We are to be authentically humble and yet exercise boldness and authority. It might really help to remember the Lord often said, "Fear not." We are not to be dominated by fear or to be shackled with guilt, but rather to be covered and governed by the unrelenting love of God. Please remember, love never fails.

Listen to the true story of a personal friend, Jordan Christy:

> Victory was at hand. I could feel it. I had just been healed from a three-year battle with Lyme disease, and God was daily giving me faith to believe I would not live a life completely crippled by rheumatoid arthritis. Life was looking up! That's why I was shocked to find myself knocked down by sheer intimidation from the enemy.
>
> God had called me to start a new ministry; however, simply filling out nonprofit tax forms quickly became a massive battle

that made Lyme disease look like a walk in the park. I would collapse into bed at the end of each day—discouraged, defeated and completely beaten up. The enemy was screaming in my ear all day long telling me how worthless, incompetent and unqualified I was. Every night I would pray that God would give me the strength to simply survive another day.

One Sunday while driving to church, I said to my husband through tears, "I am completely exhausted from fighting every day, all day. I don't know if I can take it anymore!"

My husband, a police detective, began to explain the process that law enforcement officers go through during their training at the academy.

"They line you up and go down the line, one by one, screaming in your face and telling you how weak and how stupid and how unqualified you are for the job," he said. "It seems cruel, but instructors know that if you can't handle that stuff in a controlled environment, you will never survive on the streets."

I shrugged. "Yeah . . . so?"

"Instructors can't actually put their hands on you or harm you," he went on. "Their strategy is to mentally intimidate you, physically wear you out, and emotionally break you down by pointing out all your flaws and getting you discouraged enough to quit on your own terms."

I sat there, still not understanding.

"That's what the enemy is trying to do to you," he said. "He can't touch you or harm you; his only tactic is to discourage you enough so that you will quit on your own terms." I was stunned; he was right. Seeing this new perspective changed everything. Suddenly, I was no longer a victim to cruel intimidation tactics. I was simply a rookie in training.

He reminded me of one final point: "If trainees want to make it through the academy, they can't let themselves get distracted. Fix your focus straight ahead. Don't look to the right or to the left or at what other people are doing. Keep your eyes on the prize."

That sounded familiar: "Let your eyes look directly forward, and your gaze be straight before you. . . . Do not swerve to the right or to the left; turn your foot away from evil" (Proverbs 4:25, 27 ESV).

To make a long story short, the tax forms got out and Fairhaven was born. We've already seen women saved, healed and set free. Praise God!

Jordan Christy is a wife and mother, and the author of *How to Be a Hepburn in a Kardashian World*. She has been featured everywhere from the *Today* show to the *London Times*. In those months of her illness, God reformed her identity and reminded her of who she was and what He had called her to do.

Do Not Fall for the Lies

As Jordan learned, we have to know how to stand our ground and not give in to the enemy's intrusion into our lives. Listen to the advice from the various translations of Ephesians 4:27: "Do not give the devil a foothold" (NIV). "Neither give place to the devil" (KJV). "And do not give the devil an opportunity" (NASB). This verse occurs directly after the admonition to "'be angry, and do not sin': do not let the sun go down on your wrath" (verse 26). The Greek word used at the end of verse 27 is phonetically *top'-os*, meaning "place, region, opportunity" (Strong's Concordance). In other words, the enemy, who is the accuser of the brethren, looks for opportunities to get up close and personal.

We are not to share common ground with the enemy. Satan's weapons operate through fear, doubt, self-pity and shame. Through these deceptive tactics, he tries to pry open the door of our hearts and minds and entangle us in places where we have been set free.

Our enemy is not the creator of anything. He perverts, manipulates and puts an evil spin on people and experiences. He even tries to warp how we see the Lord. There is a marked difference between the accuser's diabolical judgments and the Holy Spirit's conviction. The dark side drives us into a corner and mounts a tormenting scenario as if there is no way out. The Holy Spirit woos us to turn away from sin in repentance and turn to the Savior for redemptive grace and freedom.

Paul writes, "If God is for us, who can be against us?" (Romans 8:31). A few verses later he asks another question: "Who shall bring a charge against God's elect? It is God who justifies. Who is he who condemns? It is Christ who died, and furthermore is also risen, who is even at the right hand of God, who also makes intercession for us" (verses 8:33–34).

The accuser often will mock and malign with impressions like "You always make that mistake!" or "You never do that right!" He works through strangers as well as through family and friends. He uses circumstances such as financial trouble, shame or embarrassment as viruses of fear. The enemy wants to move pressure around by aligning one person against another, using jealousy and selfish ambition as levers. His goal is that you see only other people's faults while others see all of yours. Provocative words cause toxic emotions to arise so that they get locked in our minds and memories.

The enemy uses your bad decisions, broken experiences and past sins to contaminate your present life. That is why you must wield courageously the sword of the Spirit, which is the Word of God (see Ephesians 6:17), to demolish strongholds. You must be transformed by the renewal of your mind (see Romans 12:2) as a part of an ongoing lifestyle of courageous Christianity.

Jesus receives the ultimate affirmative prophecy as He is being baptized. A voice from heaven declares, "You are My beloved Son; in You I am well pleased" (Luke 3:22). But even after that glowing word of affirmation from His Father, Jesus is tested. After forty days, when He is hungry physically from fasting, the devil taunts Him. "If You are the Son of God, command this stone to become bread" (Luke 4:3). If the enemy has no fear of lying about the truth of who Jesus is, do not be surprised when he lies about the truth of who you are in Jesus Christ your Lord. Do not fall for the lies.

God's Military Strategy

You do not have to read far into the Old Testament where the exploits of kings and commanders are recorded to note that God, the commander-in-chief, often used unconventional methods for fighting and winning battles. One of the most unique is found when King Jehoshaphat was facing war with several kings whose armies greatly outnumbered his.

> Then the Spirit of the LORD came upon Jahaziel the son of Zechariah . . . and he said, "Listen, all you of Judah and you inhabitants of Jerusalem, and you, King Jehoshaphat! Thus says the LORD to you: 'Do not be afraid nor dismayed because of this great multitude, for the battle is not yours, but God's.'"
>
> 2 Chronicles 20:14–15

To their great surprise, he went on to tell them that they would not need to fight in this battle. "'Position yourselves, stand still and see the salvation of the LORD, who is with you, O Judah and Jerusalem!' Do not fear or be dismayed; tomorrow go out against them, for the LORD is with you'" (verse 17).

King Jehoshaphat listened to his spiritual advisor, bowed his face to the ground with all the inhabitants of Judah and Jerusalem and worshiped the Lord. The next morning, they gathered in the Wilderness of Tekoa, where they again praised and worshiped God. The king encouraged his people with these words: "Believe in the LORD your God, and you shall be established; believe His prophets, and you shall prosper" (verse 20).

Then the king presented the most unusual battle plan they had ever heard of. A choir would precede the army singing praises to the King of kings. Their song would consist of only one verse: "Praise the LORD, for His mercy endures forever" (verse 21). That was it. No weapons brandished. No loud battle cries. No storming the battlefield. Only this one line.

This does not sound very much like a Mel Gibson *Braveheart* warfare plan to me. I mean, picture Winston Churchill sending the London Symphony Orchestra to Germany to fight the Nazis. It makes no sense in the natural; however, this was a supernatural strategy—a prayer and praise strategy.

As the singers began to sing praises to the Lord, He went into action setting ambushes against the people of Ammon, Moab and Mount Seir. The enemies were utterly defeated. The only military action that was left was to strip the dead bodies of their valuables. After three days of gathering the spoils of war, what they acquired was almost more than they could take away. They returned to Jerusalem with joy, singing and playing stringed instruments. "And the fear of God was on all the kingdoms of those countries when they heard that the LORD had fought against the enemies of Israel" (verse 29).

I was awakened about three o'clock one December morning in 2018 with an impression of a few contemporary examples of when intercession changed the tide of a national crisis. I made note of a couple powerful examples.

In October of 1962, President John F. Kennedy was presented with the most serious crisis in the history of the entire world at that time, the Cuban Missile Crisis. Through U-2 spy planes, our military intelligence photographed more than forty Russian nuclear missiles being installed by possibly 3,500 Soviet military personnel in Cuba, a mere hundred miles from the state of Florida. This would give Russia a first-strike capability that would destroy the United States.

The military scenarios being suggested to the president by the Joint Chiefs were terrifying, yet seemingly necessary. The assassination of Fidel Castro was a consideration. Political diplomacy was no longer an option, as time was running out. It would be a matter of only a few days before the missiles would be operational, at which point Russia would be holding a nuclear gun to our heads.

There was a global response when JFK announced this crisis to the nation and the world. Immediately, crisis-intercessory prayer teams sprang up that were united in one cause. At the last minute, the United States sent out an armada of military vessels to form a naval blockade between Cuba and the influx of more Soviet vessels. This was language Premier Khrushchev could understand, and a nuclear holocaust was averted. But I believe it was the intercessory prayer across the globe that moved the hand of God.

In this instance, President Kennedy's moral character and his political party affiliation were not factored in. People were praying for his office as president asking God to give him wisdom and a strategy from above to avoid horrific death and disaster. It gave me a fresh and deeper understanding of how we are commanded to pray for those in authority so that we can live in peace.

Many years later, in 2001, the infamous 9/11 attack occurred in America that drove many to their knees. Sporting events were canceled. Flights were canceled or rerouted. Thousands poured into churches to pray. I was scheduled to speak at a conference in Minneapolis on September 12, but with the entire nation still reeling from the recent disaster the meeting had to be postponed until the 14th.

At the conclusion of the conference, the city of Minneapolis turned over their stadium and their security force to us free of charge for a corporate time of prayer. It was a solemn, highly emotional and significant prayer gathering in the Metrodome. We may never know what was prevented or what was initiated by corporate, intercessory warfare prayer.

Prophetic Strategy for Spiritual Warfare

The enemy's strategy is to discourage you from pursuing and following God's plan, especially if you are pressing in to do what you believe He wants you to do. As he did to my friend Jordan (whose testimony I shared earlier), Satan endeavors to smother you with lies and distractions in an attempt to drown out the voice of the Lord in your life. Nothing from the enemy can stop God from speaking. He will always communicate His encouragement to see His Kingdom provide victory for you over your adversary.

The Bible cites various graphic examples of prophetic strategy for the bold and the brave. Second Kings, for example, records a story about a pending military battle with the people of Moab who were in revolt because they had to pay tribute to the king of Israel. The kings of Israel, Judah and Edom joined forces to face Moab. After a seven-day march in dry desert conditions, they still had found no water for their men or their animals.

They had not consulted God for spiritual direction concerning His will for this military engagement, but the fear of being defeated overwhelmed King Jehoshaphat, the king of Israel, and he asked suddenly, "Is there no prophet of the LORD here, that we may inquire of the LORD by him?" (2 Kings 3:11). One of the servants of the king of Israel said, "Elisha the son of Shaphat is here, who poured water on the hands of Elijah" (verse 11). Jehoshaphat then declared, "The word of the LORD is with him" (verse 12).

When Elisha arrived, he did not trust any of the pagan kings. He saw them as ungodly, pseudorepentant leaders who were causing evil to come on his people. But in deference to good King Jehoshaphat, he called for a minstrel. When the musician began to play anointed music, Elisha heard from the Lord and shared the strategy he received by prophetic revelation.

Despite the lack of wind or rain, the military men were to dig ditches that would be filled divinely with water to service the soldiers and their animals. Elisha then prophesied, "This is a simple matter in the sight of the LORD; He will also deliver the Moabites into your hand" (verse 18).

When the sun rose, the Moabites thought that the ditches were filled with blood. They assumed that the kings of their enemy fought each other and died there, so they rushed in thinking that all they had to do was strip the bodies of the spoils for their possession. Instead, the armies of the three kings defeated the Moabites as the Lord promised.

One tactic of spiritual warfare is to divide and conquer; however, regardless of how the Holy Spirit leads, stay plugged in to Him in order to have the strategic direction for victory.

The Power of the Word

Having a true biblical foundation is vitally important.

> For the time will come [has come] when they will not endure sound doctrine, but according to their own desires, because they have itching ears, they will heap up for themselves teachers; and they will turn their ears away from the truth, and be turned aside to fables.
>
> 2 Timothy 4:3–4

False teachings and false doctrines are not new, but there is new language, and there are trendy concepts that are deceptive. Pluralism or multiple paths toward God are popular heresy today. The Word of God and the Spirit of God agree that there is only one true and wise God. Jesus is the way—not Jesus and multiple ways through other beliefs. A new atheism has also arisen that attempts to replace the eternal God with science and intellectual arrogance.

I get energized around the anointed teaching of the Word of God because the Word is deep within my heart, and it never becomes old or outdated. "You shall know the truth, and the truth shall make you free" (John 8:32).

When You Sense the Presence of the Enemy

What are you supposed to do when you sense the actual presence of the enemy? I will try and summarize a valuable life lesson from personal experience.

For some time, Barbara and I had expressed to each other our desire to go to Israel. Out of the blue someone gifted us with an all-expenses paid trip to the Holy Land. Immediately upon arrival while stepping off our tour bus, Barbara broke her ankle. Not twelve hours after arriving in Israel, we had to fly home to Texas for surgery. It was a bad break that required a stainless-steel plate and nine screws. What followed was six weeks at home with her foot elevated above her heart in my recliner that I used to watch football on TV. I had to scurry around trying to take care of her and our four children.

After six weeks of filling the roles of home health care and childcare provider, I was able finally to travel again for my ministry. I was stressed and exhausted, and yet I was also motivated to do a good job for these people I had never met. On the flight, I tried to calm myself by reading the emergency plans for crash landing—that is how desperate I felt.

It was then I had a vision. I saw a figure in a court jester's costume at such a distance that I could barely see him. There was no mistaking his fiendish little voice, though.

You're not ready; you're not prepared; you're not good enough; you can't do it!

The vision then shifted, and I saw a rickety card table with a soggy toasted cheese sandwich on a stained paper plate. Just after that, the scene dissolved, and I found myself seated at a king's table that was set with gold plates and adorned with a silver candelabra. In this palatial mansion, I was served the finest of food.

Another voice in the vision spoke gently and tenderly.

When you sense the presence of the enemy, look for the table, for God has set a table before you in the presence of your enemy. I felt an immediate lift of relief and confidence as a sharper sword was now in my belt of truth.

If you sense the presence of the enemy, do not panic. Do not listen to his voice—it will only grow stronger and louder. Your enemy will appear larger as he tries to bully you out of your place in the Lord. Stop, sit and receive from God the delicacies He wants to serve you from His table of strength, power and authoritative love. "Submit to God. Resist the devil and he will flee from you" (James 4:7).

The Full Armor of God

The apostle Paul closes out his beautiful letter to the churches in Ephesus using a description of the Roman armament of the day. He begins like this: "Finally, my brethren, be strong in the Lord and in the power of His might. Put on the whole armor of God, that you may be able to stand against the wiles of the devil" (Ephesians 6:10–11). He then proceeds to list out the important pieces of the armor:

The Helmet of Salvation. The helmet protects our minds, our thought lives and our imaginations. This battleground is especially vulnerable in our conscious state.

The Breastplate of Righteousness. Our vital organs—the heart, lungs, kidneys, liver and stomach—are covered by the breastplate. The righteousness referred to here is not our righteousness. It is the righteousness of God in Christ Jesus. That is why a self-righteous person is doomed to failure, condemnation and open assault from the enemy. We have spiritual bravery only because our testimony stands upon Jesus as the righteous one.

The Belt of Truth. The Roman soldier's belt was thick and sturdy, much like our modern weight lifter's belt. The soldier's armor was fastened to this belt. For spiritually brave believers, the whole truth about the Gospel of the Kingdom of Jesus Christ our Lord secures us for our success in battle.

The Shoes of the Gospel of Peace. Our feet are shod with the Gospel of the preparation of peace. This indicates that the soldier for Christ has been trained and prepared ahead of time. A modern comparison would be the phrase *boots on the ground*—rough and ready and in position to engage with our ministry assignment.

The Shield of Faith. This is a large full-length shield of protection that stops the flaming arrows of the enemy before they can strike our body armor. Our faith is not a secondhand experience. Operating in the Spirit of revelation releases the faith by which we stand.

The Sword of the Spirit, which is the Word of God. The sword is our offensive weapon. God's Word should be in our hearts and should flow out of our mouths with courageous understanding, knowing who we are as joint heirs with Jesus. Paul says that we should pray "always with all prayer and supplication in the Spirit, being watchful to this end with all perseverance and supplication for all the saints" (Ephesians 6:18). I believe that praying in the Spirit and declaring the Word under that anointing causes the enemy to flee.

Remember, you are never alone. The Lord has promised to always be with you. "The LORD is with me like a dread champion; therefore my persecutors will stumble and not prevail. They will be utterly ashamed, because they have failed, with an everlasting disgrace that will not be forgotten" (Jeremiah 20:11 NASB). You can be brave spiritually because Jesus, the dread champion, is always with you standing strong.

The greatest manifestation of courage in the midst of adversity is the incomparable love of God on the cross. Remember always that love never fails. Knowledge puffs up and pride blows up, but love builds up. The objective of our fight is not to conquer people, but to destroy the works of the evil one and to set people free. How different are the ways and the wonders of our God, who is our Commander-in-Chief!

MEDITATION: Bible Promises for Courage to Fight

"Do not be afraid or discouraged because of this vast army. For the battle is not yours, but God's."

2 Chronicles 20:15 NIV

Yet in all these things we are more than conquerors through Him who loved us.

Romans 8:37

I have fought the good fight, I have finished the race, I have kept the faith. Finally, there is laid up for me the crown of righteousness, which the Lord, the righteous Judge, will give to me on that Day.

2 Timothy 4:7–8

For further reading: 2 Corinthians 2:14; John 16:33.

PRAYER for Courage to Fight

Heavenly Father, I come before You having my trust established in You. You are the Lord strong and mighty. You are the Lord who is mighty in battle. Give me the power and grace to go courageously forward wherever You shall send me. With thanksgiving for the victories in Jesus, I will be strong and carry out great exploits. In Jesus' name, Amen.

ACTIVATION

- Memorize the full armor of God in Ephesians 6:13–18 and put on every piece of armor:
  - » the Helmet of Salvation that protects our minds and our thoughts
  - » the Breastplate of Righteousness that guards our hearts
  - » the Belt of Truth that binds us together and stabilizes our beliefs
  - » the Shoes that help us to walk in peace carrying the Gospel to the world
  - » the Shield of Faith that through prayer the Holy Spirit provides power to fight our battles
  - » the Sword of the Spirit that is the Word of God and our only offensive weapon
- Ask the Lord for the gift of discernment of spirits so that you will be able to recognize the voice of the accuser.

DECLARATION

I am protected by the full armor of God. This armor is able to keep me from the evil one.

COURAGE TO STRENGTHEN YOURSELF

To live in courage requires encouragement. And sometimes the only one to encourage you is you.

Bill Johnson, pastor, Bethel Church, Redding, California

In recent years it has become common knowledge that healthier food, regular exercise and the reduction of stress make for a longer and stronger life. In the same way, our spiritual lives will always need maintenance. We need genuine interaction with the Holy Spirit. We cannot just listen to self-help pep talks from trendy motivational speakers. We must learn how to use skillfully the keys the Lord provides for us. Those keys are

1. Identifying Jesus, the Christ, the Son of the Living God (see Matthew 16:16). As Peter did this, Jesus, in turn, confirmed Peter's identity and promised him success and authority.

2. Knowing your identity. You are a child of God. Knowing who you are and staying in relationship with Him and His promises is a foundational key. You are spirit, soul and body. It is important that you nurture and care for all of your faculties and that you remain in alignment with the Holy Spirit, the Word and His Body.

3. Preserving primary relationships. If married, maintain strong ties with your spouse and children. Nurture others in your intimate circle of friends. Love one another. Love covers, love edifies and love perceives what is good. Love never fails.

The following is a true story about a person whose courage was needed as he faced his personal Red Sea. These are Jordan Rubin's words from an interview that I conducted with him:

Many things in my life have necessitated the courage to strengthen myself, but this one sticks out to me. In the summer of 2008, I had just written a television program called *Perfect Weight America* and was finishing a six-month book tour. I experienced some pain in my groin that I believed was a sports hernia; however, something told me I needed to get this checked.

I ultimately had tests and exploratory surgery. It was not a hernia at all. It was metastatic cancer. I was basically a ticking time bomb! I asked my local doctor if I could handle this naturally. That is my background and my personal belief—naturally and also supernaturally.

The doctor used a bit of profanity to make his point with my wife and me. "Don't *blank* around with this. If you don't get conventional treatment, you will be dead within ninety days. There is a 100 percent chance you will be dead in ninety days."

You hear about people receiving a terrible prognosis, but this was ridiculous. I looked at him and said, "God is going to heal me."

The doctor referred me to Harvard. Before going to Boston, I underwent three weeks of intense nutritional detoxification therapy, expecting some improvement after that. At Harvard, I had blood tests that would indicate cancer activity with this particular tumor. My previous blood markers had registered 230. When the Harvard oncologist read the latest results to me, they were significantly higher. I sensed darkness and began rebuking those figures.

The doctor seemed like an undertaker delivering the bad news. But the Holy Spirit was refusing to let me be dictated to by what was written on that paper. What was I going to believe? Mickey, that's a good example of finding a way to strengthen myself. I did it through rebuking what the natural world would call the "truth" about my diagnosis. Then I walked out of this renowned medical institution with my wife. That began a journey that lasted forty days.

I committed my life to the Lord in every way possible—physically, mentally, spiritually and emotionally. I went on an entire healing program. I prayed prayers I learned from great Bible teachers—prayers that avail much. I kept talking about my healing and about the blood of Jesus running through my veins. I devoted ten to fourteen hours a day to living in a state of healing, and during those forty days, I had more joy and peace than most people who don't have a death sentence over their lives.

Every two weeks, I had a repeat blood test, and despite the fact that I felt like I was walking on water the other thirteen days, my hand was shaking when I recognized the doctor's phone number. "Jordan," he said, "I don't know what's going on here. The blood marker number was 280, but I'm getting 38, 32 and 40, tested three different ways."

I made my next appointment and left determined to fight, committing my life to prayer, only speaking the Word of God. I disconnected from work and told my team, "God has healed me, but no work. You won't see me for a while."

Two weeks later, I got a call from the doctor, my hand shaking again. He says, "I have great news, but before I read your results . . . "

Doubt crept in, and I thought, *I wonder if that last result was real?*

Then he said, "Jordan, I have your three blood test results here: The numbers are zero."

Praise God! I couldn't wait to call my family . . . but then, Mickey, that little doubt springs up: *What if it was someone else's blood test?*

No! I will rejoice! I called my parents, and I called my wife's parents. This was the amazing news we needed.

My friend who is a physician, a man who has cowritten some books with me, was not satisfied with the report, though, and wanted to make sure. He is a wonderful man, but not a believer. He said, "I will not recommend you undertake this course of action [the natural approach]. But if you insist, I'll write a prescription for a CT scan."

"I'm healed," I said, and he just looked at me. "Jordan, if anyone can say that, it is you."

Two weeks later, I had my final test, which happened to be at the end of forty days. Again, it was 000! Praise God!

Wouldn't you know, after all these amazing reports, I begin to look online to check out the statistics of people who have zero on their blood score but still have tumors. Why do we do that? Why do we refuse to fully believe? When I looked online, I found some conflicting and depressing info. I had told myself never to do this again! I'm not a statistic! I'm more than a conqueror! But . . .

I went through with the CT scan. I went through that tunnel, praying in the Spirit, believing God that this tumor was gone in Jesus' name. My wife and I celebrated, knowing that the results were to come in a couple of days.

However, the morning I was to go to the imaging center to get my final results, I was sitting at our kitchen table holding a glass of water. I started to think about the results and . . . *what happens if there's still cancer?* I had promised my wife, who also believes in natural methods, that if in forty days I wasn't healed, I would do whatever was needed to follow conventional treatments even though God had already healed me of major incurable diseases in the past. I was committed to her because I did not want to make anything my idol, and whatever God needed to use to heal me would be okay with me.

I sat there, shaking, and the glass fell out of my hand onto the floor and broke! *Lord, I believe! Help me in my unbelief!* An interesting statement because how can you believe, then ask for help with your unbelief?

When we walked into the imaging center, every action seemed to be in slow motion. I can still remember the woman behind the desk pulling out the manila envelope and handing it to me. I couldn't open it there but walked into the parking lot.

Outside, I opened it and pulled out several papers. Scanning the notes and figures, my wife and I read, "tumors and lesions." I almost literally dropped to my knees in that parking lot, and then we noticed the date—it was the original diagnosis! Flipping over a few more pages, I saw "000—no tumor activity. Lymph nodes normal."

I grabbed my wife, spinning her around, and I may have screamed, "Thank God!"

The term *cancer* is scary. It's terrifying living with uncertainty day by day. My hope and yours is in knowing that you are not a number, you're not a statistic. You are an individual, a beloved, unique child of God.

If you're reading this, no matter what your giant is, you can take courage and make the decision to strengthen yourself in the Lord. Let Joshua 1:9 and Ephesians 3:20 ring true in your life. Not only will you become a conqueror, you will become *more* than a conqueror!

Jordan Rubin was fading fast from chronic Crohn's disease in his late teens. Through wisdom and power, the Lord healed and delivered him. He did it again when Jordan was diagnosed in 2008 with cancer. Jordan has written several bestselling books, including *The Maker's Diet*. He has become a health and nutrition entrepreneur, a clear and articulate communicator, and more importantly, a loving husband who is leading his family in the Kingdom ways of our Lord.

Encourage/Strengthen Yourself in the Lord

King David is certainly one of the most celebrated personalities in all of religious history. Because of the well-known story of David and Goliath, even atheists will mention him in secular settings. There is one lesser-known episode of his life story that came to my attention very early in my public ministry. Let's take a good look at this one because it holds a secret key to strengthening ourselves.

David had been on the run from his father-in-law, Saul, for about seven years, because when Saul realized David was anointed to be king and was going to replace him, Saul determined that he would kill him. When he found himself on the run, David joined other military powers and was given land in the Philistine territory of Ziklag. With his mighty men and their families and servants he created a strong army and a community complete with valuable possessions (see 1 Samuel 27).

He served the Philistines loyally, and yet when they were preparing to battle with Israel, David's loyalty was called into question. The leaders of the Philistines rejected David (see 1 Samuel 29). After attempted negotiations with the Philistines failed, David and his men returned to the camp at Ziklag. They came upon the worst possible scene imaginable. Their community had been ransacked by the Amalekites, with all of their families and servants carried off, all of their possessions looted and the entire camp burned to the ground. David was beyond distressed, and he and his men began to cry and weep until there was no strength left in them physically. As if that were not bad enough, David's men, including his trusted officers, declared that they wanted to stone him to death because they blamed him for the calamity. David was having much more than a bad day.

"But David strengthened himself in the LORD" (1 Samuel 30:6). Having lost absolutely everything, how did he do that? Some translations say David "encouraged himself in the LORD" (KJV). Rather than focus on his horrible, no-way-out dilemma, David found a way to stand at attention spiritually and be empowered by God.

The Hebrew word used is *chazaq* (khak-zak'), which is a verb that means "to fasten upon, be strong (figuratively—to encourage oneself), to be or grow firm or strengthen." The name *Hezekiah* means "Yah has strengthened" (Strong's Concordance).

We do not know exactly what David did, but it certainly seemed to work. Although he was exhausted and sick at heart, he mustered his faith and said, "Please bring the ephod here to me" (verse 7). An ephod was a vest that was required for the high priest to have before entering into the presence of the Lord. Abiathar, the only priest to survive Saul's massacre, had the last remaining ephod.

David then asks the Lord, "'Shall I pursue this troop? Shall I overtake them?' And He answered him, 'Pursue, for you shall surely overtake them and without fail recover all'" (verse 8).

With that, David and six hundred men rode off in pursuit. Catching the thieving Amalekites unprepared and partying, David and his men descended on them and defeated them utterly. As the Lord promised, they recovered all of their wives, sons and daughters, servants and possessions with no loss of life. In addition to recovering everything that was stolen, they took back the bounty of two other military victories the Amalekites had won (see verses 9–20).

The horrific stress David must have felt in his soul is hard to imagine. Although there is no description of what David did to strengthen himself that day, we do know this: David was a man after God's own heart (see Acts 13:22). It can be argued that David was the most recorded worshiper, using his instrument, his voice and prophetic words. No doubt he was able to rise up in music and song and exalt the Lord for the beauty of His creation, or to implore Him to deliver his people from their enemies. Later in his life, when personal failure would have sealed most spiritual leaders into a life of guilt and shame, he penned and sang Psalm 51: "Restore to me the joy of Your salvation, and uphold me by Your generous Spirit" (verse 12).

Many of David's songs have been turned into contemporary worship songs. Some of the songs have brought personal deliverance to a vast number of people, including me. I once sang along with a recorded version of Psalm 3 all night until breakthrough came in the morning. David wrote this song while under the intense emotional pressure of his son Absalom's betrayal. Absalom was trying to kill his father and steal his throne. Imagine that kind of torment. Yet David sang, "But You, O LORD, are a shield for me, my glory and the One who lifts up my head" (verse 3).

In this psalm, David was decreeing and testifying to the character, nature and authority of the Lord instead of focusing on the dread darkness of his circumstance. With spiritual bravery, he strengthened himself, and through his remarkable songwriting he has strengthened billions of others for thirty centuries.

A Modern-Day Move: The Call

On September 2, 2000, in Washington D.C. on the Mall, over four hundred thousand people gathered for an event that ignited a movement that has endured for nearly two decades. It was called "The Call." The inspiration for this event came through Lou Engle, a man who wanted desperately to see America turn back to God. Prayer and fasting, along with authentic corporate worship and intercession, became a united offering to the Lord. With all generations and ethnicities coming together, they represented our nation in asking for a new move of God to advance the Kingdom.

No one knew how many would come. No one knew how it would be paid for. There was no big-name advertising or any type of paid registration. There was only raw, desperate faith. Yet the nameless leaders were all in. An event of this magnitude takes bravery for multiple reasons, including the scenarios of responsibility—the physical equipment needed, the safety and security of the people and the threat of disruption by opposing factors. But it came off above and beyond all expectations. One portion of the event involved fathers asking forgiveness of their sons and daughters. This resulted in healing happening between the generations by the power of love—priceless.

One year later, on September 22, 2001, The Call Boston was held in the city where eleven days prior two passenger jets flew from Logan International Airport to take part in the worst terrorist attack in America's history. Seventy thousand brave attendees cried out passionately for America. We were the only group of people willing to risk being in downtown Boston that day. The testimony of infamy was usurped, especially by the young people who led in the worship and prayer decrees.

In city after city, this movement grew. The united cry of hearts that was manifested in these assemblies produced a corporate dynamic. Thousands upon thousands were

> strengthened with might through His Spirit in the inner man, that Christ may dwell in [their] hearts through faith; that [they], being rooted and grounded in love, may be able to comprehend with all the saints what is the width and length and depth and height—to know the love of Christ which passes knowledge; that [they] may be filled with all the fullness of God.
>
> Ephesians 3:16–19

The Power of Pentecost

It took courage for believers to assemble in Boston so soon after the 9/11 terrorist attack. In the same way, around two thousand years prior, a group of people gathered courageously and prayed in the city where their leader had been executed publicly and brutally only fifty days prior. After multiple postresurrection supernatural appearances to some of the Lord's disciples—once, to over five hundred—He told them not to depart from Jerusalem. Instead, they were to wait for the promise of the Father. "You have heard from Me; for John truly baptized with water, but you shall be baptized with the Holy Spirit not many days from now" (Acts 1:4–5).

This outpouring on the 120 souls gathered in the Upper Room, which is often referred to as the birth of the Church, marked an unprecedented dispensation of God's presence and power. It was a fulfillment of His promise. The presence of God was not in a tent or a temple; rather, the resting place of God was now *in* people and not just *on* people. We are the Tabernacle of God,

> coming to Him as to a living stone, rejected indeed by men, but chosen by God and precious, you also, as living stones, are being built up a spiritual house, a holy priesthood, to offer up spiritual sacrifices acceptable to God through Jesus Christ.
>
> 1 Peter 2:4–5

This joy of the Lord that is our strength cannot be expressed with rational explanation. There are no words sufficient to describe His glory. He is our strength and our song, and rivers of living water flow through our attempts to give expression to our love for Him.

A number of years ago, I was asked to speak at a retreat to a group of pastors, none of whom I knew. I was highly motivated to deliver a special word to them, and as a result, I was wrestling with the content of my message. About thirty minutes into my three-and-a-half-hour drive to the retreat center, I gave up thinking and played a worship album instead. Using the repeat button on my car stereo system, I sang along with two songs—practically screaming my praises to the Lord. When I arrived at the campground, my spirit was strengthened, and I was like a caged lion ready to pounce.

Any apprehension I had been experiencing had been jettisoned way back on the interstate. By the end of my message, all of those evangelical leaders in their shirts and ties were on their faces crying out to the Lord. Fanning the flame of the Holy Spirit through praise and worship can build up your inner being for zealous, courageous exploits.

After that session, I was having lunch, and the man sitting across from me asked, "Who *are* you?"

"Well . . . I'm the pastor of a little church a few hours north of here," I replied a little sheepishly.

"You are an anointed man of God," he declared.

I found out later that he was the general superintendent of the entire denomination—a denomination that did not embrace the baptism of the Holy Spirit. I am glad I did not know where I was going or who I would be addressing. If I had known, I might have tried to help the Holy Spirit go easy on these men. It takes spiritual bravery to let God use you His way—allowing a little Pentecostal blessing to break through in an unlikely setting.

You can stoke the fire within you by recalling times when you experienced God's power breaking through. Perhaps a certain Scripture or a lyric from an inspirational song or the memory of Jesus' sacrifice for you triggered a memory—like a painting drawn on the canvas of your mind. "The Helper, the Holy Spirit, whom the Father will send in My name, He will teach you all things, and bring to your remembrance all things that I said to you" (John 14:26).

Fasting for Breakthrough

The word *fast* in Hebrew means "to put your hand over your mouth." Historically, in both the Old and the New Testaments, fasting is directly connected to breakthrough. Fasting and prayer can strengthen and develop greater intimacy with God, they can inspire us to pray with the right motives, and they can give us a greater ability to hear from God. Prayer, along with fasting, can reveal hidden sin or negatives from which He can deliver us. Fasting can sharpen our faith to a razor's edge. "I have treasured the words of His mouth more than my necessary food" (Job 23:12). If we want all of the benefits listed above, we need to deprive ourselves of our necessary food occasionally. Jesus set an example of fasting for us. "And when He had fasted forty days and forty nights, afterward He was hungry" (Matthew 4:2). He also instructed that "when you fast, do not be like the hypocrites" (Matthew 6:16).

There are different types of fasts and different lengths of time to observe a fast. I believe there are "called fasts." The call to this kind of a fast comes directly from the Lord. It can be a call to an individual or to a group of people. I believe that when the Lord calls us to do this, we should enter in wholeheartedly expecting His results.

I also believe there is a "voluntary fast." This is one that we initiate because we need to hear from the Lord about a particular issue. I have seen God honor greatly this type of fasting. I believe there is often a contest in the invisible realm that must be won by including brave people who will be strengthened by prayer and fasting. In Daniel 10, the prophet shares the testimony of his 21-day fast to break a spiritual stronghold over Persia. There was such resistance from the demonic principality over this region that the archangel Michael was dispatched to help Daniel.

Strengthened in Praise and Worship

I could go on and on about the value and joy that come from praise and worship. It is a fantastic way to strengthen yourself. You get to involve spirit, soul and body. I usually want to sit in the front row or the last seat next to an aisle because I really get moving during praise and worship, and I do not want to hurt anybody.

Some of the most significant times of worship for me are when I am alone. I play the guitar, so I take advantage of that gift to worship with spontaneous words and music. "I will bless the LORD at all times; His praise shall continually be in my mouth" (Psalm 34:1). I can also redeem the time if I am traveling by car or in an airplane. We have many resources at our disposal, as all the music in the world can come out of a tiny cell phone with earbuds.

Any time is the right time to worship, and that includes times of adversity. The story recorded in Acts 16 is an example of this. Paul and Silas had cast a demon out of a woman, and as a result they were beaten and thrown into prison. Instead of whining about being cast into the cold, dark dungeon, they prayed and sang hymns while the other prisoners listened. Suddenly, there was a great earthquake. All the prison doors were opened, and the prisoners' chains fell off.

The prison guard who was sure the prisoners had escaped was about to kill himself. Paul and Silas reassured him that none of the prisoners had left. They were able to lead him to the Lord, and he in turn took them to his own house, cleaned their wounds and offered them something to eat. That night, the jailer's entire family received Jesus. Such dramatic Kingdom results came about from worship and prayer. We are strengthened by joy and comforted with peace through praise and worship.

Strengthened in Devotion

One way to be strengthened in devotion is to stay in fellowship with your church or home group to take advantage of the Word of God being taught through others. "They continued steadfastly in the apostles' doctrine and fellowship, in the breaking of bread, and in prayers" (Acts 2:42). Scripture also instructs us to

consider one another in order to stir up love and good works, not forsaking the assembling of ourselves together, as is the manner of some, but exhorting one another, and so much the more as you see the Day approaching.

Hebrews 10:24–25

Cultivating relationships and participating actively in services or Bible studies that your church offers creates opportunities for you to "stir up love and good works."

It is important also for you to learn how to increase your private, personal devotional time. Journaling in your private time will help you to remember God's goodness to you. As you write down things God reveals to you from your time in His presence, your faith is built up.

Gathering your family—or members of your church family if you are single—together to pray and study God's Word is a great way to strengthen yourself in the Lord. My wife and I enjoy moments of study and prayer together both at home and all over the world as we travel. We call it the cluster anointing. "As the new wine is found in the cluster, and one says, 'Do not destroy it, for a blessing is in it'" (Isaiah 65:8).

When we find that these disciplines to strengthen ourselves become pure joy, we see that there is no legalism or obligation in doing them. For the joy of the Lord is truly our strength. I have worked intentionally to develop deep spiritual relationships with people who gather together for the purpose of seeking the Lord and strengthening one another. Seeing the sight of their faces or hearing the sound of their voices brings immediate joy to me. Always be thankful for these things, and let's be courageously strong for the Lord and one another.

Strengthened in Teamwork

A beautiful and practical example of teamwork within the Body of Christ is when believers link arms in ministry with other followers of Jesus. A lot of people kid me by making the statement, "You know everybody!" The fact of the matter is the Lord happened to put me in partnership with some of the best ministries on the planet. That is a testimony that I need all the help I can get. Here are a couple of examples:

The first involves the prolific ministry of Mahesh Chavda. It has been my privilege to be friends with Mahesh and Bonnie and to partner with them in their ministry for more than thirty years. Together, we hosted the very first Healing the Nations conference in Cleveland, Ohio. At that conference, Mahesh had a word of knowledge about deafness. A mom and her young daughter were attending. The daughter had a promising singing career but was growing deaf progressively. They had purchased for her the most expensive hearing aids. At the conference, they responded to the Word, but we had not heard what the result of the Word had been in their lives.

The following year, we did another event with about one thousand people in attendance. After worship, something amazing happened. The mother and the seven-year-old singer marched up to the platform where Mahesh and I were standing. The mom had her daughter's hearing aids in her hands and started to tell her testimony. But before she could get much of the testimony out, the little girl began to sing "Jesus Love Me" in an operatic voice. There was no need for any preaching with the massive outbreak of healing that followed. I cannot tell you how much Holy Spirit sensitivity I learned working alongside my friend Mahesh.

The second example involves a time when I was working extensively in Minneapolis-St. Paul at an international healing conference. During one of the main sessions, Bill Johnson of Bethel in Redding, California, had a word of knowledge that God was healing someone's knees. A few people raised their hands, and one man came forward. He was moving at about half the speed of the world's slowest snail. Using two canes, he made his way to stand right in front of Bill.

This man had shared with me previously that he had a knee surgery scheduled for later that week. I gently interrupted Bill's ministry time to tell him about the upcoming surgery. Bill laid hands on the man's shoulders and spoke the words, "Jesus, heal him." The man was healed instantly in both knees.

The facility that we were in had about two hundred people in an overflow room with a TV screen. After Bill spoke his words of healing, I heard screaming coming from that room. I ran back there with a microphone. There were several dozen women in that crowd from Teen Challenge Minneapolis—new Christians who were recovering from substance abuse and were now being discipled. The lady who was screaming had been affected terribly with crippling arthritis in her knees. This woman's impossible condition was made instantly new by the same word of knowledge Bill Johnson had given. With great effort, I got her to come forward.

It was hard because about every fifteen feet she screamed, "I'm healed! I'm healed!" When I brought her to Bill and she shared her testimony, Bill and I looked at each other, smiling.

"Why don't you pray for these people who need healing for their knees?" we suggested.

She was shocked by the suggestion; nevertheless, she began to pray. Before she was done, nearly fifty people with terrible knee pain had been healed completely. Teamwork shows us that it is all about God, even though He allows us to partner with Him. Be strengthened.

Even though the apostle Paul was about to depart this earth, he had much more he wanted to share with his beloved son in the faith, Timothy. But of all the teachings, challenges and admonitions he had given his young protégé, this would be the most important: "Therefore I remind you to stir up the gift of God which is in you through the laying on of my hands. For God has not given us a spirit of fear, but of power and of love and of a sound mind" (2 Timothy 1:6–7). Other translations render *stir up the gift* as "kindle afresh," "fan into flames," "rekindle," "keep alive the gift," "keep ablaze the gift of God."

All of these various translations paint the picture of the absolute importance of being roused with the Spirit of the Lord. No matter what the future brings, the Lord is God enough for you.

MEDITATION: Bible Promises for Courage to Strengthen Yourself

By smooth words he will turn to godlessness those who act wickedly toward the covenant, but the people who know their God will *display strength and take action.*

Daniel 11:32 NASB, emphasis added

Fear not, for I am with you; be not dismayed, for I am your God. I will strengthen you, yes, I will help you, I will uphold you with My righteous right hand.

Isaiah 41:10

But I have pleaded in prayer for you, Simon, that your faith should not fail. So when you have repented and turned to me again, strengthen your brothers.

Luke 22:32 NLT

For further reading: Psalm 103:1–2; Psalm 118:14; Isaiah 40:31; Mark 12:11; Philippians 4:13; Colossians 1:11–12; Jude 20.

PRAYER for Courage to Strengthen Yourself

Dear heavenly Father, I come before Your throne of grace with confidence and expectancy that in You is all strength and power. In choosing me, You know my weaknesses and my human limitations. I will be made strong in the strength of Your might. Lord, give me the wisdom that comes from above, and lead me in the path of life that brings You glory. Let Your strength in me be the example to all that it is not by might nor by power, but by Your Spirit as You have said in Your Word. Grant me the opportunity to use Your strength to be a blessing to others near and far. Jesus went about doing good to all. So shall I. In Jesus' name, Amen.

ACTIVATION

- Prepare yourself for what lies ahead every morning and evening. Find appropriate Scripture verses that gird your loins for battle. Exercise your gifts of the Spirit, especially your vocal gifts. Pray and sing in the Spirit.

- Find one or two willing people and begin to work together in teams exercising your spiritual gifts. Believe for healing, listen for prophetic words, pray for financial breakthrough and ask for miracles.

DECLARATION

Today I will pay attention to divine nudges, spiritual signs and illumination as the Lord confirms His desire for me to participate in ministry with Him.

CHAPTER 6 ///

COURAGE TO PERSEVERE

Never give in. Never give in. Never, never, never, never—in nothing, great or small, large or petty, never give in. . . . Never yield
to the apparently overwhelming might of the enemy.

Prime Minister Winston Churchill, in an address to
Harrow School, October 29, 1941

Even when we have strengthened ourselves, challenges can arise.
There is an element of tenacity that takes a different kind of courage that we need to explore. We will often be tempted to quit right
before the breakthrough. Although we are dealing with power and
strength from the eternal loving One, we are living in the earthly
realm. Courage for the long haul is needed. God calls us to rely
on the Spirit of the Lord and all His promises not to give up or
lose our stand on the Rock.

One who persevered in the face of almost impossible odds was
Reimar Schultze. This is his story:

"Your son is a second-degree mongrel!"

These are the words Reimar Schultze's mother heard from an angry
Nazi official shortly after his birth. Reimar was born part-Jewish in

Adolf Hitler's world. The dangers escalated from there. The Schultze family had to navigate the Allied bombing raids that leveled their city and killed 600,000 civilians throughout Germany. They escaped narrowly the wrath of the invading Soviet army, and most of their family endured and survived two years in a starvation detention camp—their father and baby sister did not survive.

Listen to Pastor Schultze in his own words as he recounts his journey.

It is indeed challenging for me to cover seventy years of personal history, spanning such a vast era in space and events, from Nazi Germany to a walk with my Creator now in prosperous America. . . . It is only very slowly that my soul was awakened, first ever so dimly through divine light filtering through the morning mist hovering over human misery, and then, finally, breaking out in full brilliance at noonday, through the divine Son of all sons, Jesus the Christ.

It is a well-known fact that six million Jews perished in the German-occupied territory. But what is not well known is how the part-Jews fared under Nazi repression. . . . The part-Jews were forever living in a twilight of uncertainty. . . . Yet perhaps the main difference between my story and that of others of like experience is that my story, rather than ending with the same gloom and doom by which it started, ends with the great commanding theme that the world is not fair . . . but God is good![1]

In a 2017 seminar, Paster Schultze imparted this life lesson:

For two years, many people, including myself and my mother, lived in a single room without any sanitation. The best food we found to eat was bread covered with green mold.

It was during that time that my mother told me, "Son, you need to always be thankful."

"Thankful for what?" I asked her.

"Don't think about what you don't have. Be thankful for what you do have."

"But we don't have anything—nothing!" I said to my mother. "You have two feet and you can walk, can't you? Just be thankful." This training in thanksgiving kept me alive for those two years and for the rest of my life.

While many survivors of tragedy go through life with bitterness and regret, Reimar is full of wonder at what the hand of God has redeemed. No hype or exaggeration. Only gratitude and humility.

Once, while giving a radio address, he proclaimed with astonishing joy, "The Nazis hated us, the British and Americans bombed us, the Russians drove us out of our home, the Danes put us behind barbed wire, and the Jews did not accept us because we were not Jewish enough . . . and I forgive them all!"[2]

A lesser man would have given up long ago. But I know Reimar Schultze to be a man of purpose, integrity and courage. I spent a weekend with Reimar and his wife, gazed on his face and saw for myself the radiance of sanctified love and supernatural courage.

Do Not Give Up!

Our ability to inherit God's promises includes circumstances that require us to persevere until those promises are fulfilled. This requires both patience and supernatural courage. God grants us the ability to be patient in these times of waiting, and this patience builds our character. The courage that we receive comes directly from God. Perseverance takes a tough kind of courage. We must keep our eyes on the Lord and not grow faint or let weariness cause us to despair or give up.

If there is a perceived delay in God's intervention, we may question where God is or what He is doing, but I believe that there are rewards for us when we persevere. The love of God gets manifested in a raw but pure way that becomes treasure we store in our hearts. For me, this love has been enough of an answer, even when I have not had an answer.

Perseverance can lead to something much higher than having our immediate needs met. It can open a huge door for God's purposes to be revealed in ourselves and others. I cannot tell you the number of times it seemed that I had no choices, but then I found myself with three simultaneously. This dilemma would be followed by seeking and waiting for God's direction. Oftentimes, the most immediate and attractive thing was not the right thing or was not the Lord's choosing. Our will to persevere and the courage it takes to do so position us for His best.

All the heroes of the Bible lived lives of endurance and perseverance in the Lord. Let's look at one amazing example of this kind of spiritual bravery.

Joseph in the Old Testament (see Genesis 37–39) was the eleventh of twelve sons of a wealthy man, Jacob, and his second wife, Rachel. Jacob had a special love for Joseph, as he was born in his old age. As a young man, Joseph portrayed a work ethic and a spirit of excellence that was greater than any of his brothers. When he shared one of his dreams with them, the content of that dream caused them to despise him even more than their father's favoritism. In their jealousy, they sold their brother to traveling merchants, and they told their father that the boy had been killed.

In Egypt, Joseph was sold again to Potiphar. Joseph found favor in this man's house as the Lord blessed Potiphar for Joseph's sake. One after another, the tests of endurance came. Since he was young and good-looking, Joseph attracted the attention of Potiphar's wife, who wanted him to have an affair with her. Day after day, she used her seductive wiles on him, but he refused steadfastly, saying, "How then can I do this great wickedness, and sin against God?" (Genesis 39:9).

On a day when no one was around, she demanded that he sleep with her. Again, he refused, but she grabbed his garment as he ran off. She told her husband that Joseph had raped her, and since she had his garment, Potiphar believed her and put the obedient and godly Joseph in prison. Even there, he found favor because the Lord was with him.

While in prison he interpreted dreams concerning two of his fellow prisoners, a butler and a baker (see Genesis 40). The interpretation of the dream for the butler was a good one, and Joseph asked him to remember him when he returned to Pharaoh's court. Once restored to his prosperous position, the butler forgot all about his agreement.

Two years had passed when Pharaoh had dreams that he could not understand (see Genesis 41). When his magicians could not interpret them, the butler remembered Joseph and told Pharaoh that in his prison he held a man who could interpret dreams. Joseph was summoned. His interpretation of Pharaoh's dreams and his wise advice caused him to become the most powerful person in Egypt, second only to Pharaoh. The blessing on his life gave him the revelatory knowledge to prepare for an upcoming famine. In the process, he was reconciled to his family, and his father rejoiced over the son he thought he had lost.

Joseph's courage to persevere by using his spiritual gifts and by exercising determination not to compromise his godly character helped him to save himself, his family and the covenant of God as a Christlike forerunner of redemption. See Genesis 37–50 for more spectacular examples of his perseverance in the face of injustice and abuse.

This tapestry of redemption continues until the time of Jesus the Messiah. He fulfills all of the requirements of the Law and declares with His last breath on the cross, "It is finished!" (John 19:30) only to rise from the dead three days later. Our ultimate deliverer frees us from all slavery and redeems us unto eternal life.

The Fruit of Long-suffering

One of the fruits of the Spirit is long-suffering. Nobody would desire trials to come upon them, but all of us should be thankful that we are not left to deal with things in the natural. This manifestation of the Holy Spirit is more of a blessing than we are willing to acknowledge. As Peter explains,

> . . . casting all your care upon Him, for He cares for you. Be sober, be vigilant; because your adversary the devil walks about like a roaring lion, seeking whom he may devour. Resist him, *steadfast in the faith*, knowing that the same sufferings are experienced by your brotherhood in the world. But may the God of all grace, who called us to His eternal glory by Christ Jesus, after you have suffered a while, perfect, establish, strengthen, and *settle you*.
>
> 1 Peter 5:7–10, emphasis added

The Greek word for *steadfast* that is used here means "stiff, solid, stable, steadfast, strong, sure." In other words, spiritual courage empowers you to persevere and causes you to be firm and not shaken. Peter tells us that we can pass through suffering because of this fruit of the Spirit.

In this writing, Peter shares a powerful key to the Kingdom of God: He can care for us better than we can care for ourselves. It takes a special kind of courage to let go and release our anxieties and worries to the Lord.

Think about what Jesus says to Peter. "Let not your heart be troubled; you believe in God, believe also in Me" (John 14:1). He makes this statement right after Peter's worst collapse in his walk with the Lord, when he declared fervently that he was ready to lay down his life for Him (see John 13:37), and after God tells Peter that "the rooster shall not crow till you have denied Me three times" (verse 38).

I believe that Peter's exhortation comes out of this experience. Perhaps he also remembered that Jesus said, "Satan has demanded permission to sift you like wheat; but I have prayed for you, that your faith may not fail; and you, when once you have turned again, strengthen your brothers" (Luke 22:31–32 NASB).

In his first letter, Peter was writing to Messianic Christians who were suffering persecution and being forced to relocate in other regions. He is exhorting them and us in these words:

> In this you greatly rejoice, though now for a little while, if need be, you have been grieved by various trials, that the genuineness of your faith, being much more precious than gold that perishes, though it is tested by fire, may be found to praise, honor, and glory at the revelation of Jesus Christ.
>
> 1 Peter 1:6–7

Peter wrote this letter some thirty years after denying Jesus. But his courage to persevere saw him through the next thirty years, and he patiently endured and was an example of Jesus.

A personal point of interest: To be honest, it is hard for me to write about this suffering stuff as I have had way too much of it. People are amazed that I can have such a positive attitude and enthusiasm about life after the airplane crash that left me disfigured and in all kinds of pain. Not only that, but our oldest son was born with cerebral palsy, and he has suffered horribly. We are still praying and seeking miraculous intervention, but enough is enough! I do not mind telling you that we want relief for ourselves, for him and for all of you. But I do genuinely have the joy of the Lord. Let us focus bravely on the Lord's intervention and stand in endurance until we come out on the other side.

Improper Emphasis on Suffering

Throughout history, there has been a serious misconception concerning suffering and trials. A belief that self-induced suffering serves to subdue or mortify the flesh and is a form of penance (paying for sin) can be found throughout the ages. In extreme cases, people have practiced self-flagellation—striking themselves with whips—as a means of penance that was practiced by both clergy and laity. When the plague ravaged Italy in 1259, Raniero Fasani, the hermit of Umbria, started this ritual.[3]

Three centuries later, Martin Luther regularly practiced this and other self-abasement practices. He would go without sleep or a blanket on cold winter nights and whip himself in an attempt to atone for his sins.[4] Later, after his revelation of "the just shall live by his faith" (Habakkuk 2:4), he was set free. Luther's freedom has spread this truth to the whole world.

While contemporary Western culture does not embrace this kind of physical self-punishment, certain doctrines and precepts that have been built around fear and guilt have kept people from the truth of the goodness of God. These attempts and designs are to scare people into submission. Jesus came to free us, not to enslave us.

Another misconception is that God sends suffering and adversity to His people. Rather, He is with us in the midst of our suffering, bringing life and transformation. In no way does this mean He caused the trouble. As we draw near to God, He draws near to us. This is about relationship and not about payment. Why would the one who taught us to pray, "Deliver us from evil" (Matthew 6:13 NASB) send evil our way?

If you are in the midst of something that is troubling to you, instead of asking the question, "Why?" why not ask, "Who?" Jesus is the Who who can help you. He is the wisdom born from above, He binds up the brokenhearted, He restores our souls and leads us in the everlasting way. He is the Way. He came to give us life and that more abundantly. Abide in Him. He is the God of all comfort.

The Will to Live

The courage of perseverance is evident in the mystery of the will to live. The reason why some people persevere and recover while others succumb cannot be known clearly. In this earthly life, we are dealing with forces that are both visible and invisible. We should be very slow to pass judgment because we do not really know why people live or die. The following testimony is an encouragement for me to persevere.

While serving as a soldier in World War II, famous human rights author Alexander Solzhenitsyn witnessed terrible atrocities—acts of revenge committed against the Nazis by the Russian military. After criticizing the cruelty of the Russian bureaucrats, including their leader, Joseph Stalin, Solzhenitsyn was arrested and sentenced to a miserable penal colony where the prisoners were worked ruthlessly to the point of death. While incarcerated, he calculated there would be no end to this torturous life and considered suicide.

Then it dawned on him that someone had to live to tell the story of the inhumane treatment suffered by so many. He later won a Nobel Peace Prize for his literary works. Although he was expelled from Russia for his political views, he continued to be a voice for human rights throughout the whole world.

In his enlightenment, he turned from atheism and Marxism to Christianity, thanking God for his experience in the penal colony, where he found his purpose and his will to live. His legacy will remain as a bright light and a beacon in Russia's dark history of atheism and abuse.[5]

I have been known as an encouraging, prophetically gifted person. I will tell you point-blank, though, that I need encouragement from others no matter how proven or great my gift has ever been. One of the three pillars of prophecy is edification (building up). I have described prophecy many times as imparting spiritual bravery. This should be the lifestyle of every one of us—we all need allies of encouragement in this broken world.

I will never forget an experience I had while at the height of my suffering in intensive care. An up-and-coming, high-profile skydiving friend of mine would drive ninety miles every day to the hospital that I was in. He drove this distance before the hospital allowed him to see me—he just sat outside of the ICU. I had not known him very well or for very long, and yet he was drawn to be there for me.

The head doctor arranged for him to be on my list of approved visitors. He would come into my room and hold one of the only places on me that was not burned—my left hand—and with a rhythmic pulse, he would squeeze my hand wordlessly. It may sound strange, but all I can tell you is that I could feel energy flowing from him into me. Only later, when I was more mature in the Lord, did I have an understanding of the impartation of supernatural courage that my friend gave me by being with me.

I spent about a year in the hospital from the time of the accident, then was released for a little break in the summer. Two years later, my friend gave his heart to the Lord, and we were water baptized together. From that first visit in intensive care our lives were bound together. Remember how our Lord Jesus during His agony in the Garden of Gethsemane wanted His closest friends to be praying with Him? Never forget that we are supposed to love one another, pray for one another and bear one another's burdens.

Death Wish

Life is short. Almost everyone would agree with that statement. "For what is your life? It is even a vapor that appears for a little time and then vanishes away" (James 4:14). But for those who are suffering physically or emotionally, or for those who are questioning the very reason for their existence, life may seem endless.

They may be asking, "Why am I here? What is life all about anyway? What is my purpose?"

I have found specific answers to these questions. I was sent back from heaven for distinct purposes that require supernatural courage.

In counseling others, I have heard people say things like, "I'm so tired of the struggle. I want to go to heaven."

"This city is so dark and awful; I want to go to my heavenly city where there is no more pain or struggle."

I have even heard, "I'm outta here!"

Wanting to die is not a solution; it is an escape. We need the spiritual bravery it takes to persevere and live for the King and advance His Kingdom.

When you die, you will have free access into eternal life if you have accepted Jesus Christ as your Lord and Savior. He is the only one who will judge who is and who is not going to be with Him.

A good percentage of invitations for salvation ask the question, "Do you know that if you were to die tonight that you would go to heaven?"

Maybe a better, more complete invitation would be, "Do you want to live for Jesus for the rest of your life to fulfill the purpose for which you have been created? And do you want to possess the courage to persevere as a disciple, reaching and influencing others with the love and power of God and the Holy Spirit?"

I want to be able to say with integrity what Jesus declared, "I have glorified You on the earth. I have finished the work which You have given Me to do" (John 17:4). Do not wish to die or quit before your time, but rather persevere bravely and run to win. "For He is not the God of the dead but of the living, for all live to Him" (Luke 20:38).

Paul lists the values of the Gospel, the power of the resurrection and the promise of our resurrection from the dead (see 1 Corinthians 15). He also declares the guarantee of Jesus' return, His Second Coming. He tells us that our mortal body must put on an immortal body like the one Jesus has now. Even though we were born out of the dust, we will become the image of the heavenly Man. The last enemy to be defeated is death, and death shall be swallowed up in life. After Paul lists all these glorious and heavenly declarations, he gives an exhortation in the last verse that applies to every human being. "Therefore, my beloved brethren, be steadfast [persevere], immovable, always abounding in the work of the Lord, knowing that your labor is not in vain in the Lord" (1 Corinthians 15:58).

With Eyes Wide Open, Keep Looking to Him

When I was going through one of the multiple skin grafts on my damaged right hand, I had an opportunity to trust God for supernatural perseverance. It had been nearly five years since my accident, but I still had more reconstructive surgery ahead for me. Barbara and I were dating, but her father disapproved of me. He was applying negative pressure on her.

This particular surgery was performed on what was left of the first and second digits on my right hand. The plastic surgeon had grafted skin from what used to be the beginning of the palm of my hand onto both sides of the fingers. Pleased with the outcome, the surgeon left almost immediately after the surgery to fly down to the Dominican Republic to lecture in a hospital.

Toward the end of the weekend, I could feel some changes in my heavily bandaged hand. I began asking the resident in charge of my case to change the bandage. He refused, saying that the surgeon had ordered it not to be changed until Monday. I felt strongly that something was wrong, so Saturday evening after dinner I snuck around to the nurses' station and grabbed a sterile kit for changing dressings. I got caught before I could change the dressings myself.

Monday morning Barbara was supposed to come to the hospital, but instead, I got a phone call from her telling me that her father had forbidden her to come, even though she argued with him that she had promised me. Disappointed, I hung up the phone. Just then the young resident came to my room and created a sterile field to change the bandage—36 hours after I had begged him to do it.

As he unraveled the gauze, the skin grafts on both sides of my digits slid off, stitches and all. All of that work on my hand was now a failed operation. Ashamed at what had happened, the young doctor bowed his head and ran out of the room, leaving a nurse to bandage it up.

They were all silent and shamefaced as I went to their desk and asked, "Where can I go to be alone and have some quiet?"

The nurse replied quietly, "The chapel downstairs on the first floor, and I'm so sorry for what happened."

Pushing open the large, wooden chapel doors, I went to the front and fell down on my face. Everything had gone wrong. The operation was a bust due to the inexperience of this resident. They should have let me change the bandage when I knew it would have made the difference. And worse, Barbara's father had forbidden her from coming to visit at the worst possible moment in our short relationship.

From way down inside, I began calling out to the Lord.

"Can You help me? This should not have happened! Please speak to me!" I looked up at the large wall-to-wall mural that was before me. It depicted Jesus sitting on the mountainside teaching the Sermon on the Mount. Underneath the painting in large gold letters were words that the medical school had added: "Man Tends . . . but God Mends."

For five years, I had endured operations and surgical procedures. I had been in and out of different states of consciousness. Earlier in my healing journey prior to an operation, I really did not know what was happening. Now I knew what was coming. I had operation preparation down to a fine art. I could estimate both the time it would take for the procedure and the pain it would cause. I could handle that. In fact, I had developed a confidence that I could beat the clock as I often recovered far more quickly than predicted.

At this moment, however, on my face in the chapel, I realized that some of that confidence was self-centered. I had put myself in the hands of doctors, of course, but I had also taken on a cocky attitude. My confidence now shifted from the skill of the doctors to my Healer, Jesus. I saw myself putting my damaged hand into His nail-scarred one. Peace flooded me.

Looking at my bandaged hand, I told myself, "It's going to be okay." And it was.

Barbara came the next day, but I did not tell her about what had happened. Instead, I had a new quiet assurance that would continue to bolster me through all that was yet to come.

Sometimes the courage to persevere is not the brave, swashbuckling kind, but the still, small voice that whispers, "I've got you." If you are suspended somewhere in limbo waiting for your answer, keep your eyes wide open. Look for the signs. Keep looking for Jesus. You are likely to see and hear more than you could ask or think.

You are a born-again, bravehearted, standard-bearing, sword-swinging, foot-stompin', always marching forward champion for Jesus. Throw down and stand up. And never, never, never give in!

MEDITATION: Bible Promises for Courage to Persevere

My soul, wait silently for God alone, for my expectation is from Him. He only is my rock and my salvation; He is my defense; I shall not be moved.

Psalm 62:5–6

But he who endures [perseveres] to the end shall be saved.

Matthew 24:13

We desire that each one of you show the same diligence to the full assurance of hope until the end, that you do not become sluggish, but imitate those who through faith and patience [perseverance] inherit the promises.

Hebrews 6:11–12

For further reading: Lamentations 3:22–23; Luke 8:15.

PRAYER for Courage to Persevere

Lord, You are my strong tower, and I run to You and stand.
Grant me the power to keep standing steadfastly on You.

There is no rock, there is no foundation that is stronger than You. By the awesome power of Your love, You have made Yourself known to me, and You will continue to do so because that is who You are. Let my life shine as a constant beacon wherever this path takes me. Let me sing of Your love forever. In Jesus' name, Amen.

ACTIVATION

- Start recognizing God's forensic evidence—His fingerprints. These will often look like coincidences that are clearly the Lord intervening in your circumstances.
- Stay in fellowship with a core group of like-minded believers who will encourage one another in the love and purposes of God. Take Communion regularly.

DECLARATION

When you wake up in the morning, declare this aloud: I will stand strong for the entire day.

COURAGE TO USE SPIRITUAL GIFTS

Courage is not the absence of fear, but rather the assessment that something else is more important than fear.

Franklin D. Roosevelt

The operation of the gifts of the Holy Spirit is intended by God for everyone. As the apostle Paul writes to the church in Corinth, "The manifestation of the Spirit is given to each one for the profit of all" (1 Corinthians 12:7). Some people were raised in fellowships that embrace all the gifts that are in the New Testament. Some church streams teach that there is no longer the need to use some of the main spiritual gifts. Others allow certain gifts while neglecting the proper use of all the rest.

For every person, it takes not only an initial step of bravery to operate in a spiritual gift, but it takes guts to try new things and to grow stronger. Remember, the gifts are not for show or to make us feel more secure, but to help and edify others, to build ourselves up and to glorify God.

I would like to share a very dramatic example of supernatural courage in the use of the gifts of the Holy Spirit.

A few years ago, two young women had a terrifying experience. They had offered a friend some space in their home to store some large equipment. As they were showing him where the storage area in back was, a man snuck in the front door that had been left slightly ajar. When the friend left and they were alone again, the home invader confronted them.

The perpetrator tied the women's hands behind their backs, and ordered them to shut up and lie facedown on the floor. As the horror escalated, one of the women proceeded to tell the assailant what she thought of his attack.

"You're not going to do anything to us! You will not be able to rape us! You can't do what you want!"

Then they both began to speak loudly in tongues. When this evil man made a move to begin his assault, they only turned up the volume in their prayer language (tongues). At this, he stopped. Without another word, he ran from their home as if being chased.

Where did such fierce courage come from? I do not think anybody practices for life-threatening home invasions with the gifts of the Spirit. But there was a time, probably when they were a lot younger, that it took all the bravery they could muster to speak in tongues for the first time. After that terrifying encounter, though, they had increased appreciation for the gifts of the Holy Spirit.

Let's analyze what happened that night to deter this guy. First, they made decrees/prophetic declarations as to what would and would not take place. Then they released through their gift of tongues a language in the Spirit that their mind could not comprehend.

> Likewise the Spirit also helps in our weaknesses. For we do not know what we should pray for as we ought, but the Spirit Himself makes intercession for us with groanings which cannot be uttered. Now He who searches the hearts knows what the mind of the Spirit is, because He makes intercession for the saints according to the will of God.
>
> Romans 8:26–27

Spiritual bravery was activated so that their wills aligned with God's will for His purposes. In this incident, that purpose was to deliver them from terrible harm. Supernatural bravery in these two young women prevailed over the evil intent of a coward.

Spiritual Gifts

Although there are nine spiritual gifts listed in 1 Corinthians 12, other gifts are mentioned in the New Testament accounts. These gifts include the fivefold ministry offices listed in Ephesians 4, as well as what are sometimes called the administrative gifts in Romans 12. But for the sake of focus, we will look at the nine gifts in 1 Corinthians 12.

These are supernatural grace gifts that each true disciple needs to be able to successfully fulfill the mission of the Body of Christ. The Greek word for a singular gift is *charism;* the plural word in the Greek is *charismata.* These nine gifts fall into three categories:

Gifts of Revelation—word of wisdom, word of knowledge and distinguishing of spirits

Vocal Gifts—prophecy, tongues and interpretation of tongues

Gifts of Power—faith, gifts of healings and miracles

I want to operate in all of them. We need all that the Lord has provided and not just some or none. I have operated in all nine of these wonderful gifts of God at one time or other. But more frequently and freely, I have operated in a few of them for long, uninterrupted periods of time. For each of these there was a first time, and it took spiritual bravery to get started. Let's take a look at this humble beginning.

Scared to Start?

I was not brought up in a church that was active spiritually; therefore, I did not know anything about the gifts of the Holy Spirit. Even after my dramatic conversion and miraculous healings, it was a few years before I became part of a church with any life in it.

A couple of years after we were married, my wife and I began attending a very colorful fellowship that burst out of the Jesus movement. We were thrilled with the contemporary music, the nontraditional atmosphere and the passionate love of all the people in the fellowship. At some point in every service they served Communion. Before Communion was served, they instructed that visitors who were not believers were not to partake. That was really very new to me, but I could also see how vitally important it was.

This was the really unique part: The person leading the Communion service would tell the worshipers it was time for the "kiss of peace." This gave the attendees an opportunity to get things right with the Lord, to go to someone they needed to forgive or to ask for forgiveness for a relational problem to make it right. This had a profound effect on me about the truth and reality of the holiness of the Lord's table. I understood that every time I took Communion, it was to be a renewal of the cost of my relationship with the Lord and the New Covenant with God.

On one particular Sunday, from the moment worship started, I had the impression that the Holy Spirit wanted to encourage me to do something I had never done before. Every song emphasized that I must share what the Lord had done for me—how He had saved, delivered and healed me from utter destruction and hopelessness. I was petrified! I felt if I did not do it right away, I could not take Communion. Still, I chickened out when it was served. Desperate to take Communion, I confessed my disobedience to the Lord and took it anyway.

Every point that the preacher made in his sermon confirmed deeply what I was supposed to do. Even the announcements were convicting me to share my testimony. But I did not know when or how was I going to find a way to do it.

As everybody was being released, I stood up and said, "Wait a minute, please. I've got something to say."

The whole group—about 250 people—turned to look at me. Then I shared about a 45-second testimony of what the Lord had done for me and how I should tell it to the whole world. The people burst into explosive praise like nothing I had seen in this fellowship. I sat down, trembling and crying, and someone put a comforting arm around me.

At the time, I did not realize what was happening. In retrospect, it was spiritual bravery that was pushing through the mounting intimidation that had been weighing me down. It would mark the first time I shared a public prophecy, which is the most common and appropriate form of prophecy in the New Testament church (see 1 Corinthians 14).

Secondly, I was making a prophetic decree about my own life and spiritual calling. For the rest of my life, I was going to be sharing prophetically my personal testimony that would accomplish multiple results, including powerful evangelism, the building of faith to create an atmosphere for healing and personal prophetic ministry. Also, I was making a prophetic decree that I was to minister all over the world. That has been true for the past four and a half decades.

I cannot tell you how much this has opened the door for my own vibrant spiritual walk. May I encourage you to never be afraid of what the Holy Spirit wants you to do. Just do it!

Facing the Giants

When does it become easier? Years of experience in operating in the gifts will not alleviate challenging moments of truth. You will still need to walk in supernatural courage since you are dealing with issues in the natural world. After several years of ministry and leadership in our local church, my being used in the gifts of the Spirit has become a frequent occurrence and mutually edifying for all the people. Even still, there are moments when I need courage.

At one time, an emotionally troubled mother of a committed young couple in our fellowship overdosed on drugs intentionally. She was found unresponsive on a walking path in a state park and was twice resuscitated en route to the hospital. I rode to the hospital in a car with two other pastors to pray with her family. The first report we received stated that the woman was on total life support and in critical condition. As we pulled into the hospital parking lot, the other two pastors began to discuss how to counsel the family concerning funeral arrangements.

Suddenly, something rose up in me and I pounded my fist on the bumper of the car, shouting, "This is a total rip-off by the enemy! This should not happen!" The other two pastors looked at me in surprise, but we were all aware of how grim the situation was.

At the woman's bedside in intensive care we saw that her skin was ashen, her body was cold and there was no movement or any other signs of life.

I anointed her with oil and prayed simply, "Lord, we need a miracle like you did for Lazarus." I then asked the Lord to raise her up, completely healed and without brain damage. This was contrary to the rational mind and without any knowledge of medical science, of course.

Two days later, we got the report that the woman had awakened, completely healed and normal! A notable miracle had taken place. It did not happen because of anyone's experience. God is more glorified when He is the only answer, and it will always take supernatural courage. But hear this: *You* can walk in supernatural courage.

Learning, Practicing and Fine-Tuning

What if I'm wrong? What if it doesn't work? Is it really the Holy Spirit, or is it just me? This is the rapid swirl of thoughts that can crowd and confuse your mind when you are endeavoring to move in any of the gifts of the Holy Spirit. It is not always tormenting fear that we are dealing with, but rather rational thinking about the natural circumstances.

How did the apostle Peter move past the consequences of getting out of the boat to walk on water? He was a professional fisherman with verifiable knowledge of people who had drowned in the Sea of Galilee. He said simply, "Lord, if it is You, command me to come" (Matthew 14:28). Ask the Holy Spirit, and then step out and walk on the water. There are no absolute experts—only other learners and followers.

I attended a large leadership gathering where the speaker was a man I knew. I had a lot of respect for his ministry. After praise and worship, I got a download of prophetic information I thought I was supposed to share. In that moment when the opportunity began to arise, I started to examine myself.

Am I going to prophesy to be impressive? Is this really the Holy Spirit, or am I just putting two and two together because I know a lot about this topic? What should I do? What should I do?

While I was wrangling with myself, the opportunity passed, and the speaker started his message. From the beginning of his message, it was all about the prophetic word that I was supposed to have given—even some keywords that the Spirit had downloaded to me verbatim. I stopped taking notes and began to repent. It did not get any better. As I continued to listen to the message, I knew the prophecy would have been a perfect fit. Everybody would have known it was the Lord.

Then the Lord spoke to me in His still, small voice: *I saw you squirming, and I knew you would chicken out. I'll give you plenty of opportunities to do it better next time. Let it go.*

I smiled and thought, *What a cool Shepherd I have. He wants to teach me His ways to move in the supernatural.*

As you develop confidence in using spiritual gifts, remember that the Lord is always teaching us deeper and better ways.

Spiritual Courage to Speak for God

You may not live in a country where it is illegal or dangerous to share the good news of the Gospel of the Kingdom, but there is always enough potential adversity in the spiritual realm to intimidate even the strongest person. That intimidation can keep you from going forth boldly where you have never gone before.

In the early time period of the New Testament Church in Jerusalem, the Bible records that Peter and John were taken into custody by the captain of the Sadducees (see Acts 4). This took place after the miraculous healing of the crippled man at the Beautiful Gate, where five thousand new believers were added to the church. Under interrogation, they were asked by what power and authority they were able to perform this miracle.

Peter, being filled with the Spirit, said earnestly,

> "Rulers of the people and elders of Israel: If we this day are judged for a good deed done to a helpless man, by what means he has been made well, let it be known to you all, and to all the people of Israel, that by the name of Jesus Christ of Nazareth, whom you crucified, whom God raised from the dead, by Him this man stands before you whole. This is the 'stone which was rejected by you builders, which has become the chief cornerstone.' Nor is there salvation in any other, for there is no other name under heaven given among men by which we must be saved."
>
> Acts 4:8–12

As the hypocritical rulers and elders observed the courage of Peter and John and understood that they were uneducated and untrained men, they were amazed and began to recognize them as having been with Jesus. They were also distressed and concerned about the outcome of the notable miracle. They counseled among themselves and determined that Peter and John must not be allowed to continue preaching in the name of Jesus.

Confronted with this news, Peter and John boldly replied, "Whether it is right in the sight of God to listen to you more than to God, you judge. For we cannot but speak the things which we have seen and heard" (verses 19–20).

After having been threatened but released, the two brave disciples returned to their friends, who rejoiced that they were free. They prayed these words: "Now, Lord, look on their threats, and grant to Your servants that with all boldness they may speak Your word" (verse 29).

This was prophetic intercession and a decree to God that they would not stop preaching the Gospel of Jesus Christ. Included was a courageous exhortation and expectation that signs and wonders would accompany the preaching of the Gospel. There was then a second corporate outpouring of the Holy Spirit. The place where they were assembled together was shaken, "and they were all filled with the Holy Spirit, and they spoke the word of God with boldness" (verse 31).

When we are filled up with Him, we cannot help speaking out—no matter the circumstances or possible consequences. For these disciples, the bravery to preach under serious threat brought both a greater unifying of the Church and another corporate outpouring of the Holy Spirit. The Church went forward from Jerusalem throughout the Roman Empire and eventually around the world.

Boldness in Today's World

Jesus said, "Behold, I send you out as sheep in the midst of wolves. Therefore be wise as serpents and harmless as doves" (Matthew 10:16). As followers of Jesus, we have confidence (courage) in knowing that we are ambassadors who are sent by the King of kings and the Lord of all. We are to be wise but not arrogant, and we are to have a humble and gentle spirit that is not contentious or quarrelsome.

We are always on a mission. We have a purpose to reach people with love and power. The rules of engagement are, "As you go, preach, saying, 'The kingdom of heaven is at hand.' Heal the sick, cleanse the lepers, raise the dead, cast out demons. Freely you have received, freely give" (Matthew: 10:7–8).

Believe that you will possess the spiritual bravery to know what to say if you are trapped in enemy territory. "Do not worry about how or what you should speak. For it will be given to you in that hour what you should speak; for it is not you who speak, but the Spirit of your Father who speaks in you" (verses 19–20).

I have never known anything to be more effective than a gift of the Holy Spirit in operation to overcome misunderstanding and outright hostility. I cannot tell you how many times the Holy Spirit has taken over a conversation that was contrary to the Kingdom and, instead, brought love and power.

Barbara and I were once on a cross-country flight from Dallas to Boston to speak at a worship conference. We happened to be seated in the first-class cabin, where our cabin mates, most of whom looked like successful businessmen, were joking with the flight attendant and making some off-color remarks.

While flying over the state of Ohio, I pointed out to Barbara where she used to live. We noticed a cloud of steam billowing out of a manufacturing plant that was located to the west of her family home on Lake Erie.

Overhearing our conversation, the well-dressed gentleman sitting across the aisle was the first to speak to us. "My company designed and built that plant."

"Amazing!" I replied. "My wife's father is the CEO of a large architectural engineering company." I named the world-class company, and he was properly impressed.

"What do *you* do?" he asked me.

"I'm a public speaker, and Barbara and I are going to be speaking at a conference in Boston."

"Really? What kind of a conference?"

"It's a worship conference. Leaders and teachers from all over the world will be there. I'll be speaking and Barbara is a worship dance teacher."

The entire first-class cabin froze as they realized they had been telling dirty jokes for almost two hours in the presence of church leaders.

After a few uncomfortable seconds, a stunned businessman said, "What? Dancing in church? I never heard of such a thing!"

We explained the concept of celebrating freely our faith using music, art, dance, drama and storytelling.

Afterward the man said more soberly, "I could feel the whole time that I was looking at you that you both were different."

The flight attendant sat on the floor as I shared my personal testimony of God's mercy to save, heal and deliver me. From 33,000 feet in the air, we continued telling spiritual stories all the way from Cleveland to Boston. Every person in that cabin, including the flight attendant, thanked us profusely when we finished.

After exiting the plane, they told us how much they had loved hearing our story. Several of them were touched by the Holy Spirit, and my wife and I spoke words of knowledge over them. These people were impacted prophetically by the content of the Kingdom message. And oh, how we loved them and thanked God for that encounter.

Jesus Models Operating in the Gifts

Without a doubt, the best example of courage in the operation of the gifts of the Spirit is Jesus. Whether in the midst of large crowds that had expectations and high hopes to receive or within an atmosphere of persecution and faultfinding, the Lord never held back to have a powerful impact on people's lives.

Let's look at some specific types of gifts and the Lord's passionate and skillful use of them.

Gift of Healing

Another time Jesus went into the synagogue, and a man with a shriveled hand was there. Some of them were looking for a reason to accuse Jesus, so they watched him closely to see if he would heal him on the Sabbath. Jesus said to the man with the shriveled hand, "Stand up in front of everyone."

Then Jesus asked them, "Which is lawful on the Sabbath: to do good or to do evil, to save life or to kill?" But they remained silent.

He looked around at them in anger and, deeply distressed at their stubborn hearts, said to the man, "Stretch out your hand." He stretched it out, and his hand was completely restored.

Mark 3:1–5 NIV

It is obvious that healing was a major part of our Lord Jesus' early ministry. After the spectacular healing of the paralyzed man in front of Pharisees and teachers of the Law, Jesus declared, "Which is easier, to say, 'Your sins are forgiven you,' or to say, 'Rise and walk'?" (Luke 5:23 ESV).

Our mission includes gifts of healing and the declaration and demonstration of our Lord's healing love.

Gifts of Word of Wisdom and Prophecy

On another occasion, Jesus came to the temple early in the morning, and all the people came to Him as He sat down to teach them (see John 8). The scribes and Pharisees brought in a woman caught in the act of adultery and set her right in front of Him. Trying to test Him and find fault, they said, "Moses, in the law, commanded us that such should be stoned. But what do You say?" (verse 5).

Jesus stooped down and wrote in the dust, acting as if He had not heard them. They persisted in trying to bait Him.

He then stood and said, "He who is without sin among you, let him throw a stone at her first" (verse 7).

He stooped down again and continued to write on the ground. The rulers' consciences were convicted, and one by one they left.

Jesus stood again and addressed the woman: "Where are those accusers of yours? Has no one condemned you?" (verse 10).

When the woman replied that no one remained, Jesus said, "Neither do I condemn you; go and sin no more" (verse 11).

Then Jesus turned to the crowd that had been listening to Him. "I am the light of the world. He who follows Me shall not walk in darkness, but have the light of life" (verse 12).

Do you see what Jesus did in this encounter? Wisdom from above ended the conflict without a single stone being cast. He followed this victory with a prophetic declaration that He was the light of the world and that His followers will always carry His light with them. It is amazing how Jesus did not get tangled up in the trap but, instead, redeemed the situation and showed that His light is superior to darkness.

Gift of Miracles

Intrigued by the signs and wonders Jesus was performing, a large crowd of five thousand men—not counting women and children—gathered around Him. Seeing the size of the crowd, Jesus asked Philip, "Where shall we buy bread, that these may eat?" (John 6:5). It was a moot point since He already knew what He was going to do.

Philip shrugged. "Two hundred denarii would not begin to pay for enough bread to have more than a few crumbs." Two hundred denarii was about the average wage of one year.

At that moment, Andrew came over to Jesus. "There's a boy here who brought a little sack lunch of five barley loaves and two small fish. Not sure it will help much, though."

"Have the people sit down," Jesus instructed. He then blessed the bread, which planted a seed of faith. And when the food was distributed, there was enough for everyone to have as much as they wanted with twelve baskets of scraps left over (see John 6:1–14).

This is one of only two miracles that are recorded in all four gospels, the second being the resurrection of Jesus from the dead. This is significant. The dialogue before and after the actual miracle is prophecy that testifies about who He is and the cost of both discipleship and eternal life.

Beyond Our Ability

It must have been mind-boggling to walk with Jesus and note the obstacles He encountered, yet also experience the joy that followed miraculous results. I guess it is safe to say that as we walk with Jesus the initial thought of hindrances and difficulties could be overwhelming; however, the joy of operating in His supernatural gifts is worth any risk.

Barbara and I were invited to be the main speakers at a large conference on the other side of the world. Four thousand people gathered for nine days in circus tents in this highly organized event. We were really honored to be there as part of a powerful ministry team.

At the end of an evening service where the presence of the Lord had been so strong, I walked down the main aisle to the back of the tent. As I reached the end of the aisle, forty or fifty people on both sides of me began to manifest spiritual oppression simultaneously— contorted faces, groaning, shrieking. These manifestations were going to require a really long deliverance session.

Shocked and overwhelmed, I thought, *This is too big. It's going to take me a long time, like I may have to move here to this foreign country to get all this done.*

Then something rose up inside me. The gift of faith bubbled up, along with an unearthly level of confidence and courage.

I said boldly, "In Jesus' name, silence!" At that, they all fell down in piles on top of each other as if they were dead.

Feeling led to continue, I commanded the evil spirits, "Leave these people! Get out of this region! Leave this country, and I send you before the Lord, and He will dispense with you!"

Instantly, the people all stood up and began worshiping God.

What I learned was that the supernatural is beyond our ability every time, whether it is one person and one nudge from the Holy Spirit or a large gathering in which more than one hundred people are affected simultaneously. It is all about the power of the Lord. Never take credit for what only God can do.

It is important to note that this event had been covered in prayer by a huge number of people for over a year. Also, the presence of the Lord that night was tangible, and the ministry leaders who hosted the event operate in a gift of fervent faith to see their entire nation changed.

You are a called follower of Jesus. As a true disciple, you are on a mission. Go boldly and bravely!

> Go therefore and make disciples of all the nations [all ethnic people], baptizing them in the name of the Father and of the Son and of the Holy Spirit, teaching them to observe all things that I have commanded you; and lo, I am with you always, even to the end of the age.
>
> Matthew 28:19–20

There is plenty of room in the Book of Life for everyone's names. Preach Jesus. He commands His disciples to preach, heal, deliver, equip, train and release people to advance the Kingdom. John Wimber, leader of the Vineyard Church movement, lavishly and joyfully did just that, initiating so many leaders and groups of people worldwide in "doin' the stuff."[1] The stuff that Jesus did.

MEDITATION: Bible Promises for Courage to Use Spiritual Gifts

But you shall receive power when the Holy Spirit has come upon you; and you shall be witnesses to Me in Jerusalem, and in all Judea and Samaria, and to the end of the earth.

Acts 1:8

Pursue love, and desire spiritual gifts, but especially that you may prophesy. For he who speaks in a tongue does not speak to men but to God, for no one understands him; however, in the spirit he speaks mysteries. But he who prophesies speaks edification and exhortation and comfort to men.

1 Corinthians 14:1–3

Most assuredly, I say to you, he who believes in Me, the works that I do he will do also; and greater works than these he will do, because I go to My Father.

John 14:12

For further reading: Mark 16:20; 1 Corinthians 14:15; James 5:14–15.

PRAYER for Courage to Use Spiritual Gifts

Gracious Holy One, we come boldly before Your throne of grace asking for that which You have promised. We ask that we would operate bravely in Your gifts with manifestations of Your Holy Spirit's power. It is when Your signs and wonders are being manifested that they are signposts that point to You as the source. Let us boast only in You. Help us to help others have spiritual bravery and confidence in the use and operation of these marvelous gifts. We thank You in advance for the opportunity to give away freely what You freely give. In Jesus' name, Amen.

ACTIVATION

- Read Scriptures about operating in the Holy Spirit and personalize them with your name. For example, (your name) went out, healed the sick and delivered people from demonic oppression, and they returned rejoicing (see Luke 10:17–19).
- Expect and receive specific directions from the Holy Spirit today. Then pray for others as you engage in the supernatural work of God.

DECLARATION

I will take advantage of opportunities God gives to me to grow in the gifts of the Holy Spirit.

COURAGE TO SUCCEED

I am still far from being what I want to be, but with God's help I shall succeed.

Vincent van Gogh

When we meet people who are successful, we might think they are built that way. We can believe that whatever they are going to do, they have the confidence, the *chutzpah*, to do it. In contrast, I believe that supernatural courage is different. The Spirit realm is unearthly. God does not call us to what we can do, but rather what we cannot do—without Him. The assignments our Lord has for us are the most ambitious and oftentimes the most precarious endeavors of any human experience.

Let's look at a man who has known both natural and supernatural courage that led to success in both realms.

> After the death of Moses the servant of the LORD, it came to pass that the Lord spoke to Joshua the son of Nun, Moses' assistant, saying: "Moses My servant is dead. Now therefore, arise, go over

this Jordan, you and all this people, to the land which I am giving to them—the children of Israel. . . . No man shall be able to stand before you all the days of your life; as I was with Moses, so I will be with you. I will not leave you nor forsake you. Be strong and of good courage, for to this people you shall divide as an inheritance the land which I swore to their fathers to give them. Only be strong and very courageous, that you may observe to do according to all the law which Moses My servant commanded you; do not turn from it to the right hand or to the left, that you may prosper wherever you go. This Book of the Law shall not depart from your mouth, but you shall meditate in it day and night, that you may observe to do according to all that is written in it. For then you will make your way prosperous, and then you will have good success. Have I not commanded you? Be strong and of good courage; do not be afraid, nor be dismayed, for the LORD your God is with you wherever you go."

Joshua 1:1–9

The Lord told Joshua four times in three verses to be strong and courageous. Joshua had to accept this assignment in the shadow of the life and ministry of Moses. God was calling the younger man to do even greater exploits than his mentor. It was up to him to lead his people out of the wilderness and to inhabit successfully the Land of Promise. Supernatural courage is the empowerment to seek to live victoriously.

God Has a General Call for Every Follower

Joshua's courage in defining moments was preparation for what was to come. At any given time, I doubt that he knew where the Lord was taking him. We may as well get used to it. God gives us the information that we need, but we must trust Him even without the complete story laid out for us.

Every true disciple needs to know Him and make Him known. I believe that increasing in our knowledge of Him is more experiential than methodical. This knowledge comes from an active, real relationship with communication and passion. To make Him known should not be out of obligation, but rather out of compassion for others. When we discover something wonderful and valuable, we will not want to keep it to ourselves. We will want to share it.

Here are some foundation stones:

1. Learn to hear and follow His voice (see John 10:27).
2. Be devoted to apostolic doctrine (the Bible) and the ministry of the Word.
3. Stay in fellowship with other believers.
4. Pray often.
5. Be His witness (see Acts 8:4).
6. Be fruitful.

Fruitfulness is the successful production of Spirit-empowered activity through bold (brave) expression (see John 15:5). Obedience to the call of God will lead you to help advance the Church.

God Has a *Specific* Call for Individuals

When God calls you to a particular assignment or to a life commitment of service, do not hesitate to accept the challenge. The following are a few biblical men who accepted that challenge.

Gideon

Recorded in Judges 6 is an account of the oppression of the children of Israel by the Midianites and the Amalekites. After the Israelites had sown their fields, they were raided and stripped of all their sustenance.

As Gideon was threshing wheat and attempting to hide it from the Midianites, the Angel of the Lord appeared to him. "The Lord is with you, you mighty man of valor!" (verse 12). Gideon responded by singing the blues. "If God delivered us why are all these bad things happening to us?" Then the Lord turned to him and said, "Go in this might of yours, and you shall save Israel from the hand of the Midianites. Have I not sent you?" (verse 14). Gideon whined, "How can I even save myself? We are from the weakest clan, and I am the lowest rung on the ladder in my father's house." And then the Lord said to him, "Surely I will be with you, and you shall defeat the Midianites as one man" (verse 16).

It took some convincing before Gideon was ready to accept the fact that this was God's word directly to him, but through a supernatural event—burning of a sacrifice—he relented. When he was commanded to tear down the altar to Baal, he obeyed timidly by doing what was asked of him at night. Even then he was not convinced that he would be able to "save Israel from the hand of the Midianites." He put out a couple of challenges to God, asking Him to prove His intentions, and received indisputable proof— today we would call it a confirmation.

The Lord's next instruction was baffling to him. He was to whittle down his army of 32,000 eager warriors to a mere 300. That strategy was intended to remove any doubt that it was God who provided the victory. And you know the rest of the story— the Midianites were routed thoroughly that day. Glory to God!

Most successful believers give Him the credit for any success they enjoy. Gideon was certainly one of those. He responded to the call. While Gideon never considered himself capable of such a feat, the Lord had called him "a mighty man of valor." It is time we accepted God's estimation of us, knowing that He will provide the capability equal to the calling.

Peter

This firebrand of a disciple was called to transition from a Galilean fisherman, who was plying his trade on the Sea of Galilee, to a successful fisher of men, who would affect millions around the world. In his first solo preaching assignment (see Acts 2), he successfully hauled in three thousand new believers—not bad for his first day on the job. If he had refused, he would have missed out on the birth of the Church.

Paul

He walked the journey from former zealot to preacher, teacher, apostle and prophet. He took a definite climb up the supernatural ladder. Paul's anthology of courageous acts would require an entire book to do justice to this superhero of the faith.

However, in the world's eyes, his adventures might have seemed anything but successful.

> I received forty stripes minus one. Three times I was beaten with rods; once I was stoned; three times I was shipwrecked . . . in journeys often, in perils of waters, in perils of robbers, in perils of my own countrymen, in perils of the Gentiles, in perils in the city, in perils in the wilderness, in perils in the sea, in perils among false brethren; in weariness and toil, in sleeplessness often, in hunger and thirst, in fastings often, in cold and nakedness.
>
> 2 Corinthians 11:24–27

Yet, despite all the delays, setbacks and outright attacks, he considered himself to have succeeded. He told his spiritual son Timothy, "I have fought the good fight, I have finished the race, I have kept the faith" (2 Timothy 4:7). He shared that he was anticipating the "crown of righteousness, which the Lord, the righteous Judge, will give to me on that Day, and not to me only but also to all who have loved His appearing" (verse 8).

There are some false beliefs that could hinder people's efforts to succeed. The idea that poverty equals spirituality is one example. For some people, any material gain—whether that is one's home or their transportation—calls into question a person's character as not being authentically spiritual. Such criticism could be expected from those in the world, but it is tragic when those in the Church judge and criticize other Christians because of some success or gain. I know personally some of today's most prominent ministers who have been castigated by other high-profile believers—who do not know these people or their private lives—because of their external wealth. They disregard their noble character and selfless charitable deeds.

That goes for some businesses, too. In today's world, there are several notable companies that have held firm on the courage of their convictions. Chick-fil-A and Hobby Lobby are among them. Their continued success in maintaining spiritual principles has been an example to all of those in the business world that God is faithful.

Yes, there are stories of moral failure in business enterprises and ministries in the Kingdom. These get a lot of media attention because bad news gets front-page space. What is often not seen are the millions of success stories of hardworking, faithful people who pour their lives into the Lord, their families and their communities and who never ask for or expect their fifteen minutes of fame. I know many of the personal stories of successful ministries that are led by some of the most charitable and unselfish individuals.

Forward Steps and Full Stops

There are seasons in the lives of all—both individuals and groups—who are called to serve the Lord. As it takes supernatural courage to launch a new endeavor with the Lord, it also takes bravery to recognize a change of season or transition. "The steps of a good man are ordered by the LORD" (Psalm 37:23). I also believe that the *stops* of a righteous man are ordered by the Lord. It is difficult to transition from something that is bearing fruit for the Kingdom to take on the unknown. Spiritual maturity, however, brings sensitivity to discern what God is doing, even when it does not make sense to the natural man.

Take Philip, for example. The fired-up young evangelist was headed to Samaria to preach Christ to the multitudes. That's a good many more than a few dozen. And what about the response to his message?

> With one accord [they] heeded the things spoken by Philip, hearing and seeing the miracles which he did. For unclean spirits, crying with a loud voice, came out of many who were possessed; and many who were paralyzed and lame were healed. And there was great joy in that city.
>
> Acts 8:6–8

At the height of one of the most successful regional evangelistic outpourings in the book of Acts, Philip was instructed by an angel to leave the region and "go toward the south along the road which goes down from Jerusalem to Gaza" (verse 26). This is smack-dab in the middle of the desert. Most people who had just experienced a successful crusade would want to start more churches, blast it out on social media, have multiple campuses with big-screen preaching, bring in the hottest worship bands and advertise: The revival is located right here! Instead, without further instruction, Philip obeys the Holy Spirit and takes off for this desert place. Obedience opens the door for the advancing Church to walk through.

Out in the middle of nowhere, Philip saw a man in a chariot. The Spirit then said, "Go near and overtake this chariot" (verse 29). As he got closer, Philip heard the man reading from the prophet Isaiah: "He was led as a sheep to the slaughter" (verse 32).

"Do you understand what you are reading?" Philip asked.

The man, an Ethiopian of great authority, replied, "How can I, unless someone guides me?" (verse 31).

The Ethiopian then said, "I ask you, of whom does the prophet say this, of himself or of some other man?" (verse 34).

The teachable moment all evangelists dream of happened for Philip.

"Then Philip opened his mouth, and beginning at this Scripture, preached Jesus to him" (verse 35).

Following that impromptu sermon, they came upon some water.

The Ethiopian said, "Can I be baptized?"

Then Philip said, "If you believe with all your heart, you may." And he answered and said, "I believe that Jesus Christ is the son of God." So he commanded the chariot to stand still. And both Philip and the eunuch went down into the water, and he baptized him. Now when they came up out of the water, the Spirit of the Lord caught Philip away, so that the eunuch saw him no more; and he went on his way rejoicing.

Acts 8:37–39

Then from the city called Azotus (Ashdod), Philip "preached in all the cities till he came to Caesarea" (verse 40).

Did you follow that? Let's take another look at Philip's divine itinerary: He starts preaching in Samaria, is told to stop and go to the desert, finds one person, leads him to the Lord and baptizes him, disappears and arrives in another city, preaches there and in all the successive cities until he arrives in Caesarea. Now that is a success story, a story that is punctuated with illogical obedience.

When we were based in our home church in Butler, Ohio (population 800), I was privileged to be the pastor. Our church had more diversity than the bar in *Star Wars*. Great worship, gifted teachers and preachers, two pews of former Amish; two pews of a Spirit-filled motorcycle gang, resplendent with colors; and just about every other kind of a person in between. A few years later, I was asked to join with three other ministers to design and administrate a prophetic conference. We did not even know what a conference was, but we were going to do it anyway.

I found a venue at a university in the town where we lived. Our first conference was attended by about 250 people, but the presence of the Lord was beyond measure. We decided to do another conference the following year, and the attendance nearly doubled in size. By the third year, having moved the conference to Cleveland, we maxed out a hotel ballroom with one thousand people in attendance. After that, we had to move it to Toledo, where we exceeded two thousand people every year.

One of the most gratifying aspects of the process were the relationships we forged. Though Barbara and I moved from Ohio to Texas before settling in Nashville, we continued to lead this conference with our team and many affiliated ministries that followed. As other doors were opening for Barbara and me, we were led to turn the annual conference over to the team, even though it had been such a vital part of our lives and ministry. It was difficult to make a decision like that when such power and love seemed to be at the peak of productivity. But we had a great run, thanks be to God. Trusting the Lord and letting go is a major part of laying hold of what the Lord has for us.

We Reflect, Not Deflect, the Glory of God

We do well to honor people for their godly accomplishments, as long as we do not exalt anyone except the Lord Jesus. Like the moon, we reflect the light of the sun (Son). In Jesus' High Priestly Prayer of John 17, He prays for us: "The glory which You gave Me I have given them" (verse 22). In fact, if we deflect instead of reflect the Light of God, we miss an opportunity to honor Him.

When we refuse to recognize actions that are successful, we hinder the expression of God in our lives and quench the Spirit. Jesus rejoiced greatly when the disciples came back and reported that they had success in healing and casting out demons. We should not be afraid of God's blessings and rewards. Instead, we should expect to receive from the Lord, and in doing so, we should avoid the false belief that if we are blessed with something good, something equally bad will follow. "The blessing of the LORD makes one rich, and He adds no sorrow with it" (Proverbs 10:22).

Though it is good to honor people and rejoice with them, we need to exercise caution when inserting our own opinions. Many people think the phrase "Mind your own business" means something like "Keep out of my way." Actually, this colloquialism should be used literally. The actions we engage in need to be focused on our personal responsibilities and priorities. We should be telling ourselves, "Stay in your own lane," and, "Don't compare yourself with others."

Many of us have an opinion about what other people should be doing or not doing. Peter shows us an example of stepping into that pitfall.

"When you were younger, you girded yourself and walked where you wished; but when you are old, you will stretch out your hands, and another will gird you and carry you where you do not wish." This He spoke, signifying by what death he would glorify God. And when He had spoken this, He said to him, "Follow Me."

Then Peter, turning around, saw the disciple whom Jesus loved [John] following, who also had leaned on His breast at the supper, and said, "Lord, who is the one who betrays You?" Peter, seeing him, said to Jesus, "But Lord, what about this man?"

Jesus said to him, "If I will that he remain till I come, what is that to you? You follow Me."

John 21:18–22

As serious as this reality was concerning Peter's own martyrdom, Jesus was saying, "Mind your own business." I am sure Peter never forgot the Lord's words, especially when it counted most.

As I write this, my wife, Barbara, is asking me, "Are you going to tell them how to become successful?"

I would say playfully that we should leave that answer to the self-help guru section of the bookstore, however, the Bible is full of wisdom and promises on how to be successful. The Lord our God is the only one who can truly judge who is or is not successful at what He has called anyone to do. Jesus said, "This is the work of God, that you believe in Him whom He sent" (John 6:29).

Wherever you are in your life, it is not too late. You can do something significant. Do not look back. Look down at your feet and tell them to walk straight into the goodness of God to see Him glorified in everything you do. Dream big, swing for the fence and run to win. May you be blessed with much favor from the God of wonders. You are called to inherit a blessing.

MEDITATION: Bible Promises for Courage to Succeed

"But seek first the kingdom of God and His righteousness, and all these things shall be added to you."

Matthew 6:33

Yet in all these things we are more than conquerors through Him who loved us.

Romans 8:37

My God shall supply all your need according to His riches in glory by Christ Jesus.

Philippians 4:19

For further reading: Deuteronomy 8:18; Isaiah 40:31; Romans 8:37.

PRAYER for Courage to Succeed

We come before You to ask that You would grant us all of the wisdom from above, the special grace and the specific anointing we need to be successful in our lives, in our callings and in all of our endeavors. Let us first aspire to be successful in relationship with You. Grant us the courage to have ambition—godly ambition and not selfish ambition. We also ask that You would provide the energy, spirit, soul and body empowerment to do the work that You give us. Holy Spirit, give specific discernment for various assignments. Show us the people who You have assigned to work with us, and give us the wisdom to say yes and no at appropriate times. Show us the power and provisions that You have available for us to be victorious. Lord, help us to be most successful in our primary relationships—spouses, families and our intimate circle of friends. Let us be successful in our love for You, our love for one another and our love for the work. It is a good work, and You are a great and marvelous God. In Jesus' name, Amen.

ACTIVATION

- Review and recite Bible promises that pertain to you.
- Recognize that God is choreographing time, resources, people and circumstances for your success.

DECLARATION

I am expecting to inherit blessings from my heavenly Father and believe that this is God's will for me.

COURAGE TO FORGIVE

You must totally forgive them. Until you totally forgive them, you will be in chains. Release them, and you will be released.

Dr. Josif Tson, former president,
Romanian Missionary Society

Utilizing supernatural bravery to forgive is not entry-level work. The ability to forgive is a continuation of the character development of the lives that we have as new creatures in Christ (see 2 Corinthians 5:17).

How do we get to a place where we have the courage to forgive others? How are we able to get the release that the Lord intends for us to have within the challenges that we face?

The truth is that it is not usually within our natural ability to forgive. We need the supernatural help of the Spirit of God. Where the Spirit of the Lord is, there is freedom, peace and joy.

We all have times we struggle. Listen to the wisdom of a man who is a highly respected theologian, a man filled with the Holy Spirit:

The wrong I believe was done to me affected just about every area of my life. . . . I felt at times like Job when he cried, "I have no peace, no quietness; I have no rest, but only turmoil" (Job 3:26). . . .

I was . . . filled with so much hurt and bitterness that I could hardly fulfill my duties. . . . I had only told Josif of my problem because I thought I would get sympathy from a man I deeply respected and whom I thought would be on my side. . . . But no! . . . Then came those remarkable words—spoken in his Romanian accent: "You must totally forgive them."

"I can't," I said.

"You can, and you must," he insisted. . . .

It was the hardest thing I'd ever been asked to do, but it was also the greatest thing I had ever been asked to do.

An unexpected blessing emerged as I began to forgive: a peace came to my heart that I hadn't felt in years. . . .

This feeling lasted for several months, but eventually I lost it. . . . If I allowed myself to think about what those people did, I would get churned up inside. I would say to myself, "They are going to get away with this. This is not fair! . . ." and the sweet peace of the Lord left again. . . .

I had to make an important decision: Which do I prefer—the peace or the bitterness? . . . Having been on both sides, I can tell you: the peace is better. The bitterness isn't worth it.[1]

What God did for me, he will do for you. . . . Chances are you have a story, if told, far outweighs mine in terms of unfairness and hurt. I reply: the greater the suffering, the greater the anointing and blessing—if you truly totally forgive them. Your life will change . . . and, most of all, you will be blessed with extraordinary grace and freedom.[2]

R. T. Kendall was the pastor of Westminster Chapel in London, England, for 25 years. He has written more than 60 books, including this ground-breaking book on forgiveness. I have had the privilege of hearing R. T. speak in public meetings, in small-group sessions and in personal conversations. Of all of his many and varied notable ministry assignments, his premier life message is contained most aptly in the above quote. Open your heart to the Lord to see the light of revelation that is bringing freedom to you.

Me, Myself and I

It is really easy to become offended. There are many injustices, some of which are hard to even speak about. Those who offend us have their own issues to deal with. But regardless of how they handle their side of things, it is our responsibility to process our issues. We have the power residing in us to untangle these messes and sweep them away.

My wife, Barbara, and I have four adult children—three boys and a cute little caboose, our only daughter. We also have seven grandchildren—but discussing all of them would take another whole volume.

I have already mentioned our oldest son, Michael, who was born with a diagnosis of cerebral palsy. *CP* is a broad term. In his case, it is orthopedic and affects severely all four limbs and his upper torso. As eager young believers and first-time parents, we treated Michael pretty normally. He talked early, he was very loving and relational, and yet he did not develop physically at the expected time. He never crawled on all fours or got up and walked. We clung tenaciously to the belief that God would do miracles of healing for our son.

When Michael was two years old, his brother Matt was born. Three years later, Jacob, followed by our daughter, Elizabeth. Even though the other kids developed on schedule, Michael did not. He adapted in many ways as we tried to adapt as well; however, finding specific help for him in the areas of education and physical therapy proved to be challenging.

When Michael was twelve years old and attending school, it was brought to our attention that the curvature in his back needed medical evaluation by a specialist. We opted for one of the world's most famous hospitals and orthopedic pediatric specialists. This doctor was very confident that he could help Michael. He said he had performed this surgery many times with great success. After much prayer and with a little reluctance we moved forward with this corrective surgery. The incision was from the base of his skull to the end of his spine. Two metal rods with wires and screws were inserted to hold his straightened spine that had been pulled straight by an appliance similar to an automobile jack.

When we were able to see Michael in the recovery room after surgery, he was in enormous pain and had lost the ability to control his bladder. We were assured by medical staff that all functions would return. They told us that his symptoms were only the results of the medication and that he would be fine.

We should have suspected something when a week later they discharged us secretly out of the back service elevator. He was still in tremendous pain and had to be catheterized intermittently, a procedure with which we were unfamiliar. He lost many of the other abilities that he had before the surgery, and those functions never returned. The medical people at that institution continued to lie, to deny any responsibility or to offer any remedy. All of this was devastating to him and to our family. At the time, we were pastoring a wonderful church community in the middle of nowhere, and if it had not been for the members who stepped up and helped us, I do not know what we would have done.

I was incensed at the gross dishonesty of that world-famous medical center, specifically the doctor who had performed Michael's surgery. In the malpractice lawsuit that followed, the witnesses lied about the obvious facts. The surgeon himself lied categorically on the stand. It was the most disgraceful kangaroo court of injustice I had ever seen or heard of anywhere.

As time passed and our family moved to Nashville, Tennessee, Michael's siblings married and had children. He is still pursuing opportunities to grow and share within his range of limited abilities. I know of no one who wants to live and contribute more than my son Michael. That being said, the amount of suffering that has occurred because of this failed operation continues to haunt me. It was only through supernatural bravery that I could release the bitterness of the pain through forgiveness.

Through various stages of forgiveness, I have been able to release and forgive the doctor and the institution. There were, however, other people and circumstances of injustice associated with Michael that were outrageous. I struggled with knowing where the line was between defending your loved one who needs assistance and being an embittered vigilante who wanted some kind of justice. While entangled in this web of confusion, it was hard to discern that the offense was mine, the anger was my issue and the focus of unresolved conflict was about me. Scenarios of selfish ambition wanted to bring about vindication but not redemption.

Layers and layers have come off of me like the graveclothes wrapped around Lazarus. I have realized that vengeance and retribution are weak and ineffective. It is the anointing of forgiveness that breaks the yoke with the power of God's love and forgiving redemption. Justice is good. Mercy is better. Mercy triumphs over judgment. This is a better way of living. The Lord is freeing and cleansing His bride. He has overcome, and you are an overcomer.

Toxic Triggers

When you are buying or selling a property, you notice all of the real estate signs, and you are conscious of mortgage rates. Everything you see causes you to compare your property to other properties. Once you have sold your home and the transaction is complete, you no longer need to be focused on For Sale signs or real estate ads.

Unfortunately, when there are hurts and wounds without forgiveness, it seems like the pain is never over. Before forgiveness, when I heard the name of the famous hospital where Michael was hurt, it triggered instant negative emotions. Medical episodes that our son experienced exploded into immediate blame and anger toward that doctor and medical center. TV advertisements for malpractice lawyers that I saw brought more memories of gross injustice.

Trying to deal with these things individually was like wiping soiled spots off my clothes while working in a stable full of manure. When I worked through forgiveness and release, the triggers quit working. The thoughts and images stopped appearing. Toxic speech no longer spewed out of my mouth. The atmosphere became clean and clear, and peace began to rule in my heart again.

Try it. It will work for you, too.

Redemptive Results

The Kingdom of God is often demonstrated in the realm of contrast. Contrast between what is holy and good and what is natural and temporal.

In the book of Luke, Simon the Pharisee invites Jesus to his house for dinner. A woman in the city, a known sinner, walks into the house, goes directly over to Jesus and begins weeping. Washing his feet with her tears, she then anoints them with the oil from an alabaster flask and kisses them. Simon the Pharisee takes in the scene in stony silence.

If this man is an authentic prophet, He would know this woman's shady reputation and would never have allowed her to touch Him!

Jesus knows, but He also knows Simon's thoughts. "Simon, I have something to say to you" (Luke 7:40). He then tells a parable.

"There was a certain creditor who had two debtors. One owed five hundred denarii, and the other fifty. And when they had nothing with which to repay, he freely forgave them both. Tell Me, therefore, which one of them will love him more?"

Simon answered and said, "I suppose the one whom he forgave more."

And He said to him, "You have rightly judged." Then He turned to the woman and said to Simon, "Do you see this woman? I entered your house; you gave Me no water for My feet, but she has washed My feet with her tears and wiped them with the hair of her head. You gave Me no kiss, but this woman has not ceased to kiss My feet since the time I came in. . . . Her sins, which are many, are forgiven, for she loved much. But to whom little is forgiven, the same loves little. . . ."

Then He said to the woman, "Your faith has saved you. Go in peace."

Luke 7:41–50

At that time it took courage for any woman—particularly a woman with her history—to approach a group of men. The fact that she let her hair down in front of anyone but her husband was even more astounding. Yet her love surpassed her fear. As she washed and anointed Jesus, He washed and anointed her—then, and for all eternity.

Knowing how much we have been forgiven and experiencing the reckless love of God empowers us to forgive others. The Pharisee and the others at the table missed their opportunity to receive redemption because they did not understand this fact.

In a church where I was a leader, I had a close relationship with a member who was continually in conflict with me and many others in the church as well as other places. He insisted on meeting with me and two of the pastors. He wanted to vent his offenses and rapidly rattled them off. After about thirty minutes of this, Pastor Steve interrupted.

He said, "The Holy Spirit just spoke to me."

"What was it?" the man wanted to know.

"I'm supposed to wash your feet."

"Okay, but I'm going to wash your feet first" was his surprising response.

"No, that's not what the Spirit said to me. Just go ask the secretary for a pan of water and a towel and come back."

When he left and closed the door behind him, I burst out crying. Somehow the Holy Spirit ricocheted off that wall and hit me right in the heart.

"Something beautiful just happened here, but it was not for the person intended, was it?" asked Pastor Steve with compassion in his voice.

I had agonized over the conflict with this man, and for years I had tried to penetrate his wall of hurt without success. I had not realized how deep my frustration and hurt went. After that moment, my relationship with him would never be the same. There would not be the struggle for me to try to save or rescue him. As someone who had received so much forgiveness in my own state of weakness, I could only offer forgiveness and release him into the Father's hands.

Forgiveness for Rejection

Most everyone has experienced some form of rejection. It could be something as simple as the end of a puppy love relationship or not being chosen on the high school basketball team. Severe examples, such as never feeling love from your father, sensing you were unwanted by your mother, or a marriage ending in divorce can cause open wounds. Equally damaging are the wounds of betrayal and shame that produce similar reactions of feeling unwanted.

Society is suffering from the continuous breakdown of interpersonal relationships. People can get caught in the crossfire of others' relational problems and end up picking up secondary offenses of others.

It was in the early '80s when I heard a very gifted pastor challenge our congregation on the subject of rejection. Using many compelling Scripture verses, he convinced the congregation that rejection was sin. Virtually everyone in that audience went forward to repent. Only rebellion, denial or spiritual blindness would have caused a person not to have believed that he or she was, indeed, guilty of the sin of rejection. So masterful and inclusive was the sermon that I wanted to feel guilty and wondered why I did not.

God began to reveal to me how suffering rejection can lead to sin, but that it was not a sin. If it were a sin, that would mean that victims of child abuse, broken marriages or racial prejudice, people who were handicapped both physically or mentally, or victims of practically every type of social injustice since the dawn of time would be judged.

Not only is the concept of rejection being a sin inaccurate, it is made worse by the guilt-driven, futile, often powerless religious struggle to be set free by human efforts. Loneliness, alienation and isolation are related emotional perceptions that can rise quickly when the open wound of rejection is unchecked.

Having been a victim of severe burns, I am very aware of the danger of open wounds. Our skin, the protective organ that covers our entire biological system, shields us from all types of contamination that cannot enter without open access. My body had to be covered with skin grafts to prevent infection that would have killed me. In a similar way, untreated, open, emotional wounds can allow toxic attitudes to enter the bloodstream of your inner being. This sets you up for emotional and spiritual infections.

Father Wounds

As a pastor and counselor for four and a half decades, I have witnessed how many people's problems can be traced to a father wound. I know because I was one of those people. My biological father never said, "I love you." He never complimented me on my accomplishments; rather, he criticized me when I tried to excel in the ways in which I was gifted. His method of discipline was physical abuse that was administered with anger. He was an angry alcoholic, and I was a target. I never saw him shed a tear or show compassion for the wounded or disadvantaged, although he was very intelligent and would often share his opinions with sarcasm. I disdained my dad's image, and from an early age, I aggressively pursued a totally different lifestyle.

As a child in the '50s and a teenager in the rapidly changing '60s, I chased adventure and worldly pleasures. I lived for the moment, wanting everything immediately. Little did I know that my life was on a collision course with human mortality and a spiritual confrontation.

After my accident, due to our destructive relationship, my father was not allowed to visit me in intensive care when everyone thought I was dying. I cannot imagine how terrible that must have been for him.

It was when I was in rehabilitation that he was first allowed to visit me. It was when it was just the two of us that he spoke to me. I remember vividly his words.

"Son, how could this happen to you? I've made a mess of my whole life, but you didn't do anything to deserve something like this." He coughed and cleared his throat. "Uh . . . just a minute, I'll be right back."

He went out in the hall and wept bitterly. When he came back in, I could see that he had been crying. Actually, so had I.

"Why did it have to be like this?" I moaned. It was in those moments that I realized we cared for one another, but that care had been buried under a lifetime of hurt. Without exchanging any further words, through the work of the Holy Spirit who had forgiven me, the cleansing of forgiveness erased any offense. There was immediate forgiveness, peace and reconciliation. This may have even been a key to my accelerated physical healing.

In the years going forward, I learned about his tragic past that he had kept a secret. In comparison, the years he had been married with a family were probably the most productive and healthy of his life.

Though he did not change much outwardly, everything between the two of us changed because of the freedom that forgiveness brought.

I deserve little, if any, credit for leading my dad to the Lord. As a lifelong atheist, he received Jesus as his Savior through the unlikely witness of his landlord weeks before his untimely death. Yet, I am overwhelmed with the knowledge that for twelve years prior, he and I were completely free from all negativity and bitterness toward each other. Now, that is a miracle.

Bitter-Root Judgment

I have a long and personal relationship with Elijah House Ministries. John and Paula Sandford were founders of this modern-day, inner healing ministry of the Holy Spirit. One of the foundational truths that they operate in is discerning and liberating people from roots of bitterness.

> Strengthen the hands which hang down, and the feeble knees, and make straight paths for your feet, so that what is lame may not be dislocated, but rather be healed.
> Pursue peace with all people, and holiness, without which no one will see the Lord: looking carefully lest anyone fall short of the grace of God; lest any root of bitterness springing up cause trouble, and by this many become defiled.
>
> Hebrews 12:12–15

Bitterness can be characterized as unfulfilled revenge. This rooted offense can make a person's perception jaded—seeing things through a victimized lens. Often, the reaction does not seem to be connected to the actual trigger. Many people, for example, are wounded by things that their church did to them that were expressed in a similar way to how their fathers wounded them. It is easy for such people to deem that all churches are guilty of hypocrisy, abuse or greed.

Wounded people often say to themselves, "I will never trust those kinds of people again!" Because of their hurts, they pre-judge automatically all churches or church members, painting them with the same brush.

One of the main hints that someone has a bitter root of judgment is an almost total lack of trust in anyone or anything. Even after there is forgiveness, it takes time for trust to be rebuilt. But healing will not occur fully until the root is removed.

Where Freedom Reigns

Can a man, woman or child really be free from these snares and entanglements? What must we do to have lasting freedom?

Let's consider what we know about Christ Jesus:

> "He is despised and rejected by men, a Man of sorrows and acquainted with grief. And we hid, as it were, our faces from Him; He was despised, and we did not esteem him" (Isaiah 53:3).
>
> "He came to His own, and His own did not receive Him" (John 1:11).
>
> He was accused falsely of being born out of wedlock.
>
> His fellow synagogue members attempted to throw Him off of a cliff after He quoted the most hopeful fulfillment of prophecy and Scripture (see Luke 4:29–30).
>
> He was resisted constantly by the spiritual leadership of the day.
>
> He was doing good to all while they tried to trap and condemn Him with His own words.
>
> He endured the vilest onslaught of mental assault in the Garden of Gethsemane that was ever released against any individual. Using vast resources of thousands of years of practical experience of torment and manipulation, Satan tried to turn the Son of God away from His prophetic destiny.

And after all of that, what happened? Jesus was not only able to withstand this anguish, but He was able to overturn the greatest attack of the ages. He used a key to the Kingdom of God as He submitted to the Father: "Not My will, but Yours, be done" (Luke 22:42). With those words He paid the price to break sin off the human race. Although He was the only human to be born without a sin nature, He bore all of our sins. He became sin on our behalf. Even though the sins of humanity nailed Him to the cross, He entered a plea in the court of heaven: "Father, forgive them, for they do not know what they do" (Luke 23:34).

One might say, "Sure, Jesus could do that because He was not only man but also totally God. What chance do I have?"

Let me assure you that the healing of rejection and the uprooting of bitterness is available through the power of forgiveness. If you are a believer in Jesus, you are loved and accepted by the only one who really matters for eternity. As you have been forgiven, you have the ability to forgive others. It really does work.

The New Testament disciple Stephen was a newly appointed deacon, and as such, he was a target for persecution. When he was asked to give a defense before the high priest, he shared the way God had been present in Israel's history. He then confronted the religious leaders for being stiff-necked because of their obstinate refusal to believe (see Acts 6–7).

At that, they drove him from the city. To gain greater freedom to do their dirty work, they took off their cloaks and laid them at the feet of a young man named Saul. As they hurled heavy stones at Stephen's body, he appealed to heaven, "'Lord Jesus, receive my spirit.' Then he knelt down and cried out with a loud voice, 'Lord, do not charge them with this sin.' And when he had said this, he fell asleep" (Acts 7:59–60).

Stephen was able to forgive his murderers out of the internal resources of the Lord's forgiveness for him. This was done in the same way that our Lord forgave when He was crucified. Unbelievable! As a result, young Saul, who was both a premier persecutor and an eyewitness, was later converted. Through his many letters to the New Testament churches, he taught the doctrine of forgiveness to all people.

I was a wandering, unsecured soul who was seeking satisfaction from the approval of man and the temporal appetites of this natural world. "The eyes of man are never satisfied" (Proverbs 27:20). Abiding in the grace of forgiveness can be contagious. As we see with Stephen, when you forgive, you never know how God might use the subject of your forgiveness—or even some bystander—to change the world.

MEDITATION: Bible Promises for Courage to Forgive

And forgive us our sins, for we also forgive everyone who is indebted to us.

Luke 11:4

Bearing with one another, and forgiving one another, if anyone has a complaint against another; even as Christ forgave you, so you also must do.

Colossians 3:13

If it is possible, as much as depends on you, live peaceably with all men.

Romans 12:18

For further reading: Proverbs 28:13; Matthew 6:14–15; Ephesians 4:32; Matthew 18:21–22; Luke 6:37; Romans 8:1–2.

PRAYER for Courage to Forgive

Lord, I come before You as one who has received great grace. I thank You, Lord, that because of Your grace I have been given bold access to come before You. And it is only because of Your grace and forgiveness that I stand and walk in the light. By the joy of Your love in the power of Your Spirit, cause me to forgive others and to live in harmony. Help me to keep looking for redemption in relationships with the people I encounter. It is out of Your forgiveness that I will be able to forgive others. Thank You for the increase of this revelation. In Jesus' name, Amen.

ACTIVATION

- Remind yourself of a time that the Lord healed a broken relationship. Believe that the Lord can do it again.
- Discern people in your primary circle who need to be cleansed, liberated or reconciled. Ask forgiveness for your part of the problem.

DECLARATION

I forgive anyone in my past who has ever offended me, and I repent of any vengeful thoughts I have entertained.

CHAPTER 10 ///

COURAGE TO LOVE

It was in prison that we found the hope of salvation for the Communists. It was there that we developed a sense of responsibility toward them. It was in being tortured by them that we learned to love them.

—Richard Wurmbrand, *Tortured for Christ*

In the tapestry of human experience that is woven together with its successes and failures, love is the thread that binds. It is the one thing that is most needed. The only perfect love is the love of God. We must receive His love before we can give it away to others. If you dare to pursue Him with a burning heart, you will risk rejection, being misunderstood, and maybe even persecution. But if you find the courage to love like God loves, you will be among the bravest of all.

As someone who appreciates the work of CBN—the Christian Broadcasting Network—I was delighted to be invited as the keynote speaker at an international worship conference held at the CBN Conference Center in Virginia Beach, Virginia. Worship leaders, artists and dancers from all over the world gathered for four days. They brought their instruments, costumes, bells and whistles (literally), and they came with all the passion and expertise of highly creative people.

I was so pumped to preach I could hardly contain myself. After getting into a little foundational teaching, I ramped up with some prophetic exhortation on my topic, "Sacrifice and the Release of Power." By the end of the message, people were lying prostrate on their faces crying out to God and asking Him to help them with self-centeredness so that their worship would be authentic and their praise would be an acceptable sacrifice to Him. The buttons were practically popping off my shirt as I observed this dramatic response to my sermon.

I had hardly noticed that twice during my message an elderly man had gotten up and walked slowly out into the hall, returning a bit later to take his seat and listen to the rest of my message. After receiving many compliments on my ministry, I went over to meet this man who had wandered in and out. He and his wife had been sitting at the end of the front row.

His name? Richard Wurmbrand—the world-renowned author of *Tortured for Christ*. I tried not to show my complete shock and utter embarrassment. I had just preached a message on sacrifice in front of the man who had written the book.

He and his wife, Sabina, had been the guest speakers all week long at Regent University on the Virginia Beach campus. I was scheduled to speak again at nine the next morning. There was no way that I wanted to speak during that session, so I begged him to take my place. I wanted to learn at his feet. He consented generously, delivering a stop-the-presses message the following day.

"Oh, my little children—I can say that because I am four times older than some of you," he began. "I can also say that because, for fourteen years while locked up in prison, I prayed every day for revival in America . . . and now I'm looking at it in you."

We all listened in rapt attention as Richard shared his story of becoming a Romanian Christian minister of Jewish descent, suffering persecution and imprisonment for his faith, but refusing to deny Jesus.

> It was in prison that we found the hope of salvation for the Communists. It was there that we developed a sense of responsibility toward them. It was in being tortured by them that we learned to love them. A great part of my family was murdered. It was in my own house that their murderer was converted. It was also the most suitable place. So in Communist prisons the idea of a Christian mission to the Communists was born.[1]

Richard remained steadfast in his faith during this confinement, sharing this graphic account. "The prison guard who was commanded to come into my cell, demanding I renounce Jesus Christ, would then strike me with an iron pipe across my legs. Repeatedly I told him, 'I know you don't understand, but I love you . . . and Jesus, whom I serve, really loves you.'"

Richard had seen this prison guard killing one of the other Christian prisoners for refusing to deny Jesus, so it was a bit surprising when the guard said, "Please stop saying that! It hurts me to do this. I hate my job, but this is what they make me do. It's why I am an alcoholic."

Years later, Wurmbrand encountered this guard again and learned that he had accepted Jesus and had been imprisoned for his new faith.

Throughout his imprisonment, Richard demonstrated the greatest commandment described by Jesus: "'Love the Lord your God with all your heart' . . . and the second is like it: 'You shall love your neighbor as yourself'" (Matthew 22:37, 39).

Who is our neighbor? Picture this: You live in a subdivision and see the man next door putting out the trash or walking his dog. Because of your frequent interaction with him, you get to know much of what is going on in his life.

You often ask, "How are you doing?" or "How's the family?"

When you discover that they are dealing with some kind of problem, you might ask, "Anything I can do to help?" This is a neighbor—someone you see regularly.

For Richard, that prison guard was his only neighbor. He was the person Richard saw most frequently. He was the person who came to beat him. The neighbor Richard loved. Such brave love is so supernatural that it seems impossible; however, I got to meet the man who embodied that truth.

At the end of his message that glorious morning in Virginia, Richard asked two of us to hold up his arms so that in front of the audience he could dance before the Lord—in spite of his stiff and calcified ankles that were in that condition because they had been broken so many times. Obviously, all of us were undone by the power and passion of his courageous love. Out in the hall, as I was walking the couple back to their room, Richard stopped and turned to me.

"You know, Mickey," he said, "the only reason I survived in prison all those years is that I would pick up my chains and make music with them and dance before the Lord."

This is supernatural courage from a twentieth-century man who proved that the power of God's love is greater than tribulation, injustice or even the imminent threat of death. The evidence was observable in Richard and Sabina Wurmbrand that day as their faces glowed with holy radiance. "Love never fails" (1 Corinthians 13:8).

Courage to Love the Unlovely

On the cross, perfect love in the form of Jesus the Messiah paid a formerly unpayable debt that set the captives free—free from acting in sinful, hurtful and destructive ways.

Some may love to gamble, love to drink and party or love to be in control. Even while we were sinners, He came to give Himself away for you, me and others we know.

The Gospel (the Good News) is the power of God unto salvation. The love of God is seminal. It is the origin and the creative force of real love. The love of God is transcendent, far above human ability to be compassionate or to care effectively. To know and experience the unrelenting love of God is to know the most formidable force and overwhelming threat to the power of the dark side. Nothing else is comparable to His love in individual, life-shaping and world-changing ways.

It is hard for us to comprehend fully, but perfect love lives in all types of imperfect people, and it is working to transform them according to His image.

In his letter to the Ephesians, Paul encourages us:

> That Christ may dwell in your hearts through faith; that you, being rooted and grounded in love, may be able to comprehend with all the saints what is the width and length and depth and height—to know the love of Christ which passes knowledge; that you may be filled with all the fullness of God.
>
> Ephesians 3:17–19

God wants us to be full of Him. This means being full of courageous love for the Lord, His ways and His people. Walking by faith in the love of God empowers us to overcome the entrapment of sin's pleasure. We have a promise that the pleasure of God is far greater and is safe. Allow me to share a couple of aspects of my personal encounter with the love of God that manifested in transformation, even in my grossly imperfect state.

When my spirit returned to my mangled body, having left the manifest presence of God in the third heaven, everything was different. Though I was not aware of the theology of what had happened, I was still overwhelmed by having encountered God—something that did not make sense.

Seeing me wake up from my deathly state, the doctors and nurses surrounding my hospital bed were terrified. Even though nothing had changed for me physically, the glory that I had beheld in the purity of heaven was now inside of me. My body was still ravaged by all the deadly complications and the pain. Yet, I was experiencing perfect peace that surpasses understanding. I had a new ability to perceive supernaturally the extremely troubled hearts and minds of these five or six doctors and nurses—and I felt bad that they felt bad. I wanted them to feel better. I was experiencing a supernatural love with which I had no previous experience.

I continued to love everybody and everything. I recall hearing a doctor speak a little harshly to one of the nurses. Instead of judging the doctor, I felt compassion for both of them. I had love and empathy for their little struggle even though my life was a hopeless mess.

I was different supernaturally, but nobody had words to describe it. The power of love transcends all known languages.

Another experience of the supernatural love of God occurred early in my fledgling public ministry. Along with a small group of businessmen and ministers, I was asked to visit the Mansfield Prison Reformatory not far from where we lived in Ohio. This prison was so dark and oppressive that three Hollywood movies were filmed there, the last and best-known being *The Shawshank Redemption.*

I was highly motivated to go, even though I had never been in a prison before. After our group was processed through extreme security, I was given the responsibility of standing at the steel door that opened to the chapel to distribute tracts that shared the Gospel and biblical promises.

The chapel held a maximum of four hundred prisoners. When that steel door opened, the Holy Spirit descended on me like a cloud. As I looked at each one of those men, the love of God streamed through me. To the natural eye, most of them would appear to be the most unlovable, undesirable and unworthy human beings anywhere—drug addicts, murderers and sexual perverts. And yet for all of them, I experienced the unstoppable, unrelenting perfect love of God. This was beyond human capability. It had very little to do with me, except that I was a vessel. The power of this love was so intense that a few times I thought my chest would burst.

This is how much the Lord loved every one of those men. I knew without a doubt that this was also how much He loved every person on the planet. Overwhelmed, I sat silently and watched as fifty-plus men stood up to give their lives to Jesus at the end of the service.

A few weeks later, the chaplain called and asked if I would preach at the upcoming Sunday service. I thanked him and agreed.

On Sunday, after boldly sharing some of my testimony and the message of God's love and power to save—taking the worst of circumstances, no matter what happened, and creating good and a whole new kind of life—I gave the invitation. Another fifty-five men stood up with tears running down their faces as they received Jesus as their Lord and Savior. Most of the men in these conditions are so dead and empty inside that they have no ability to cry or release their emotions in any way. This was really a work of the Holy Spirit. He opened hard hearts and set the captives free.

A short time later I put together a rock band with three friends who were professional musicians. We went to that prison about five times a year, and each time we would see at least fifty to seventy-five men surrender their lives to Jesus.

The cloud of love that descended on me that first day was God's deposit in me for these men. As often as I would be willing to go and point them to Jesus, God used me, and the pain and broken-ness of the men would pull His love out of me. The spiritual bravery that it took for me to keep going helped me to look past the broken, tormented and demonized lives of the inmates and the corruption of the guards. I was able to see men whom Jesus loved.

Over the next six years, every Christian group that had been vis-iting that prison was kicked out—except us. The warden once took me to lunch at a restaurant in the downtown area of Mansfield.

Over lunch, he told me, "All these religious groups know that the prisons are a growth industry, but you guys are different."

I was not there for any money. That was never my motivation. My motivation was this raging love—seeing people set free from the real prison.

Courage to Love for Families

Families, whether church or biological, frame the social structure intended by God. It takes courage to commit to love, as maintaining relationships requires a lot of give and take. It takes courage to push through difficult situations while also maintaining love and kindness. We show courage when we express vulnerability in communication, when we trust those we love even in the face of having been disappointed and when we forgive both great and small offenses.

Why did Jesus teach that God was Father and refer to us as brothers and sisters or sons and daughters? Because family was His idea from the beginning. Only the enlightened and the brave will find the courage to love God's ways in a permissive society that endorses destructive pleasures.

Training your family to follow the Lord despite society urging them in another direction is a courageous act. Lead your family to spend time in the presence of the Lord, to spend time serving brothers and sisters in Christ and to reach your neighbors. Go with your family to express love and generosity to people in your community. Using your talents and abilities to bless those around you sets a beautiful example for both your church family and your biological family.

Tough Love

Tough love is a relatively modern term. It usually means speaking with harsh or strong words to loved ones in the hopes of instructing or correcting. It can mean requiring someone to take responsibility for their own self-destructive behavior. Regardless of how or why it is expressed, tough love always is motivated by love. It can be difficult at times to love those related to you. The greater the strain that is on a relationship, the greater the amount of courage it will take to love. The temptation to be defensive, to shun or to lash out in anger is unproductive. Spiritual bravery and discernment will empower you in this risky territory.

Even our Lord Jesus had this problem in His own family circle. "When His own people heard of this, they went out to take custody of Him; for they were saying, 'He has lost His senses'" (Mark 3:21 NASB). Still, He continued to love all people, including His brothers.

The Stronghold of Cold Love

It was prophesied by Jesus that things will become darker as the end times draw near, with one of the symptoms being that our love will grow cold. "Because lawlessness is increased, most people's love will grow cold" (Matthew 24:12 NASB). Earlier in the passage, Jesus tells us that the reason that many people's love will grow cold is because many will be misled. "See to it that no one misleads you. For many will come in My name, saying, 'I am the Christ,' and will mislead many" (verses 4–5 NASB).

The outworking of people being led astray will be that they will fall away from Him, they will betray one another and they will hate one another (see verse 10). Allowing our love for Jesus to grow cold causes us to act with judgmentalism and have knee-jerk reactions that can drain us spiritually and emotionally.

Saying "They deserve it," or "I saw that coming," or "They never learn their lesson" can be a litmus test of one's own spiritual condition. People such as this are not operating in love, but in self-righteousness. They have placed themselves in the seat of Moses as a judge. In a scorching rebuke to the scribes and Pharisees, Jesus said "woe to you" eight times, assailing their judgmental attitude and practices of religious hypocrisy (see Matthew 23:13–29).

Our response should be to strive to rekindle our passion and make a commitment to know the Word of God so intimately that we will not be misled. We should endeavor to make all things about Him, committing to make time to study the Word with other believers, to protect our own personal devotional time and to find ways to serve the ones that He loves. When we make things about others, passion follows.

We should also endeavor to demolish strongholds and take every thought captive (becoming aware spiritually), casting down imaginations. Having an active awareness of spiritual forces, specifically those that would try to deceive us, is paramount to keeping our love from growing cold.

Love Is an Action Word

In this life, we are told by Scripture to abide in faith, hope and love (see 1 Corinthians 13:13). Those are not only heavenly virtues, but the currency of the Kingdom. How do we keep love going, and how does it increase?

"A friend loves at all times, and a brother is born for adversity" (Proverbs 17:17). These words indicate that love is to be continual, not intermittent. "But above all these things put on love, which is the bond of perfection" (Colossians 3:14). "Put on" indicates the action of bestowing tender mercies and kindness, preferring one another. These are relational activities and expressions of genuine love.

"Let brotherly love continue" (Hebrews 13:1). This word for *love* in the Greek is a combination of the words *phileo* and *adelphos*, which together mean "brother." "And may the Lord make you increase and abound in love to one another and to all, just as we do to you" (1 Thessalonians 3:12). These words describe an active, loving lifestyle of personal interaction with others as a true follower of Jesus.

Charity Begins at Home but Does Not End There

In the New Testament of the King James Version of the Bible, the same Greek word is translated 89 times as *love* and 26 times as *charity*. In modern English-speaking nations, charity is thought of as giving to the poor and needy. Almsgiving is a definite aspect of Christ's expression of love; however, charity includes far more than giving to the needy. Acts of charity can become simply a social activity that misses the quantitative love. A person full of charity is forgiving, tolerant and lacks ulterior motives. A loving, charitable person does not draw attention to him or herself; rather, with humility, he or she gives honor to others.

In modern times, Mother Teresa of Calcutta was a profound example of true charity. Likewise, Rolland and Heidi Baker of Iris Ministries have been a beacon of light in some of the world's darkest places. Light shines brightest in the darkness, which causes the darkness to flee.

Love expressed in charitable almsgiving is not new in the Body of Christ. Consider the following account documented in the third century AD.

Although Laurence was very young, he was appointed to the position of deacon, one of seven who were serving in the cathedral church in Rome in AD 258. This was a trusted position that included taking care of the church treasury and distributing the riches of the church to the indigent. In spite of political adversity at the time of his appointment, revival was breaking out all around Laurence.

Persecution against the Christians increased under Emperor Valerian. He ordered all bishops, priests and deacons to be arrested and executed. He offered Laurence a way out if he would show them where all the church's treasures were stored. If he complied, Laurence would be free from any of the edicts the emperor had given, including execution and imprisonment.

Deacon Laurence asked for three days to gather all the treasures into one central location. During those three days, he brought together the blind, poor, disabled, sick, elderly, widows and orphans. When Emperor Valerian arrived, Laurence flung open the doors and exclaimed, "These are the treasures of the church!"

The emperor was so angry that he decided beheading was not terrifying enough, and he ordered this spiritually courageous man to be roasted on a gridiron. The young deacon's great courage as he was dying made such an impression that revival in Rome only increased. Many people, including several senators who had witnessed Laurence's execution, became followers of Jesus.[2]

Most ministries that care for the needy focus on the love of God. Some brave and Christ-centered organizations even move in the gifts of signs and wonders. Not only have they taken irrational financial risks, but their very lives are often in harm's way in order to reach people with love, care and the power of God.

God Is Love

The apostle John, often referred to as John the Beloved, wrote his last three entries in the Bible in his early 90s while in the Ephesian church. The major themes in these writings are love, light, knowledge and the value of life—love being the dominant one. Living in active love is the clear evidence of an authentic follower of Jesus. A lack of love indicates that one has prevailing elements of darkness.

The Word is very clear: "Beloved, let us love one another, for love is of God; and everyone who loves is born of God and knows God. He who does not love does not know God, for God is love" (1 John 4:7–8). He continues by saying, "And this commandment we have from Him: that he who loves God must love his brother also" (1 John 4:21).

I have already introduced you to Michael, our eldest son, who was born with cerebral palsy. Barbara and I have watched Michael endure horrible physical and emotional trials with little complaint. He is a true champion of the courage to love. The injustices he has experienced have at times driven me crazy. But our son's love for others, his spiritual prophetic sensitivity, his sense of humor and his love for life challenge me to draw upon Jesus so that I can rise above my own weaknesses.

MEDITATION: Bible Promises for Courage to Love

Love must be sincere. Hate what is evil; cling to what is good. Be devoted to one another in love.

Romans 12:9–10 NIV

Above all, love each other deeply, because love covers over a multitude of sins.

1 Peter 4:8 NIV

My command is this: Love each other as I have loved you.

John 15:12 NIV

For further reading: John 21:15; Proverbs 3:3–4.

PRAYER for Courage to Love

Lord, I realize that You know everything about me. You know my secret thoughts, my abilities and my dreams. But now, Lord, I ask that You overshadow all of me with Your unrelenting love. Compared to all that I can ask or think, You are and have been the most amazing relationship I have ever encountered. Your love has transformed me, strengthened me, spoken to me and comforted me. From Your love within me, lead me to touch others and testify clearly of who You are. Let a bridge be built between my healed heart and others' lives. When I am strained in life, let more of Your perfect love empower me to share and impart to others how amazing and fascinating You are. Let the only explanation be that I have been with Jesus. I thank You, Lord, and I expect You to flood me with Your presence. In Jesus' name, Amen.

ACTIVATION

- Seek a baptism of love by asking the Holy Spirit to pour out a stronger portion of Jesus' love upon you.
- Make a short list of people with whom you have a strained relationship, and ask God to show you powerful ways to pray for them and love them.

DECLARATION

I will look at everyone I see today through the lens of God's love and ask Him for His heart for them.

COURAGE TO GO THE DISTANCE

I want to keep taking mountains, raise up the next generations, and remain radically surrendered to Jesus with no place
for compromise all of my life. I want to stay tightly bound to
His Word, responding continually to the beckoning call of His
Spirit, embracing both His commands and His promises.

Don Finto, pastor emeritus, The Belmont Church,
Nashville, Tennessee

The legacy of our lives will be defined by how we finish our race
on this earth. The Lord never calls us to coast. He instructs us to
ask, seek and knock. Communion with Jesus—encountering Him
continually—empowers us to keep the faith. When Jesus returns,
He will have a crown of righteousness waiting for those who have
been longing for His appearing.

In the previous chapters, we looked at various aspects of how
supernatural courage causes us to go boldly where no man has ever
gone before. Our lives and the events that occur are opportunities
for us to press on and move forward. Incorporated in this moving

forward is the miraculous power of transformation—to be conformed to the image of Jesus. I am persuaded that the challenges we encounter are more about relationship with Him than actual accomplishments.

Wherever you are on your journey with the Lord, believe that as God uses you that He is also changing you. He is the Potter, and we are the clay. Hear the words of a man who is a present-day example of one who is all in to run all the way from here to eternity.

I am grieved every time I hear of a fallen pastor or evangelist, whether from a local congregation or a radio or a television ministry. This did not have to be. What happened? How did they fall from being a passionate follower of Jesus? Or had they been living a hypocritical life all the time so that eventually the crash came?

There are some places in Scripture that I dread reading because I know what's coming. I love the story of young Solomon when he ascended to his father's throne. He is the model of humility. "I am only a little child and do not know how to carry out my duties . . . so give your servant a discerning heart to govern your people and to distinguish between right and wrong" (1 Kings 3:7–9 NIV).

What an auspicious beginning! We would assume that this man might become the godliest king in all of Israel's history. Even God was impressed (see 1 Kings 3:10) and assured Solomon that his prayer would be answered. He would have a wise and discerning heart.

Solomon began with a glorious reign. People came from all over the known world to witness his wisdom and pay him homage. He oversaw the building of a magnificent temple and experienced the heavy presence of the Lord at its dedication, so much so that the priests could not even perform their service.

But fast-forward a few years and get ready for your heart to sink. "Solomon, however, loved many foreign women . . . his wives turned his heart after other gods . . . he followed Ashtoreth . . . and Molech . . . Solomon did evil in the eyes of the LORD" (1 Kings 11:1–6 NIV).

Maybe you don't remember, but Ashtoreth was worshiped with the vilest of sexual perversions and Molech was worshiped with child sacrifices.

What happened?

Solomon had not kept close to God in those intervening years. A king of Israel was to "read [the Torah] all the days of his life so that he may learn to revere the Lord his God and follow carefully all the words of this law and these decrees" (Deuteronomy 17:19 NIV). But Solomon did not keep reading the Torah.

If he had read the Torah, he would have known that a king "must not acquire great numbers of horses" or "return to Egypt to get more" (Deuteronomy 17:16 NIV). Solomon did both.

The king was not to "accumulate large amounts of silver and gold" (Deuteronomy 17:17 NIV), but "the gold that Solomon received yearly was 666 talents" (1 Kings 10:14 NIV), and he "made silver as common in Jerusalem as stones" (1 Kings 10:27 NIV).

The Torah read that "[the king] must not take many wives, or his heart will be led astray" (Deuteronomy 17:17 NIV), but Solomon had seven hundred wives and three hundred concubines (see 1 Kings 11:3).

Solomon's compromises began to harden his heart so that, in spite of all his wisdom, he died an evil, depraved idolater.

One of my friends aptly said that sin always takes you farther than you intended to go, you pay more than you intended to pay and you stay longer than you intended to stay. The biblical scribe quotes King David, who in spite of many failures did finish well—God saw him as "a man after my own heart" (Acts 13:22 NIV), saying, "Today, if you hear his voice, do not harden your hearts" (Hebrews 4:7 NIV).

One of my biblical heroes is Caleb of old, who along with Joshua, urged Israel to go in God's power to conquer the land God was giving them. The other ten spies swayed the crowd against Caleb and Joshua, resulting in a 40-year-long delay in a barren wilderness before the next generation entered the land.

When starting a ministry after years as a pastor of a local congregation, I did not choose Solomon as a model, but named the ministry "Caleb Company" for three reasons:

1. Caleb was still taking his mountains when he was 85.
   "Here I am today, 85 years old! I am still as strong today as the day Moses sent me out; I'm just as vigorous to go out to battle now as I was then. Now give me this hill country" (Joshua 14:10–12 NIV). I am a bit amused when I read that. I suspect Caleb may have been exaggerating slightly, but I like his attitude, and I intend to keep that frame of mind all my days.
2. Caleb was all about raising up the next generation.
   God had promised him that his descendants would inherit the land (see Numbers 14:24), and he knew how to do it. After all his bravado about being so fit, he knew he needed younger men in battle. "I will give you my daughter Acsah in marriage to the man who attacks and captures Kiriath Sepher [a part of his hill country]" (Joshua 15:16 NIV), He announced. Othniel took the challenge, won the battle and the bride, and became Israel's first judge.
3. Caleb is continually described as a man who "followed the LORD my God wholeheartedly" (Joshua 14:9 NIV). In other words, he did not flake out like Solomon when he got old.

I intend to be one of today's Calebs. I want to keep taking mountains, raise up the next generations and remain radically surrendered to Jesus with no place for compromise all of my life. I want to stay tightly bound to His Word, responding continually to the beckoning call of His Spirit, embracing both His commands and His promises . . . . Come, go with me!

These are the words of Don Finto, a former missionary, college professor and, for 25 years, pastor of Belmont Church when it was a member of the Church of Christ, a denomination that does not believe in the use of instrumental music in worship. Ironically, this little congregation exploded as one of the most influential fountains of both contemporary Christian music and the Jesus movement. During the time that he was at Belmont Church, Don was a pastor and spiritual mentor to the likes of Michael W. Smith,

Amy Grant and dozens of others who would become household names throughout the Christian world.

As Don navigates the river of God, he continues to be active as a primary leader with the resurrected community of Jewish believers in Jesus, both in the United States and in Israel. He was honored recently as a member of the Gospel Music Hall of Fame. Although not a singer, songwriter or musician, Don was awarded this honor because he continues to love, shepherd and encourage Christian musicians.

At a conference in Nashville some years ago, I heard Heidi Baker, the miracle-working missionary of Iris Ministries located in Mozambique, say fondly, "At nearly ninety years of age, Don Finto is the youngest person I know!"

In this last stretch of Don's life, he has become the accomplished author of three books, translated into seventeen languages to date.[1] His inspirational legacy of the written and spoken word will continue to influence people all over the world.

I have had a supernatural connection with Don Finto that began thirty years ago at a strategic conference in Kansas City. I could never have imagined how the power and the purpose of God would have been manifested through that divine appointment. Even more impressive than his refined and unique wisdom are his passionate hunger for more of the Lord and his resolute zeal to see the fulfillment of all of the vision the Lord has shown him.

Way to go, Don. Thanks for giving me the opportunity to walk with you and the fond memories that I will cherish forever.

Who Am I . . . and What Am I Doing Here?

Everything has taken a new direction for those who have come to know Jesus as the Lord of their lives. All decisions and actions should now be determined by the leading of the Holy Spirit. We who have come into authentic relationship with God through salvation should know what we were saved from—a godless life—and what we were saved to—heaven and eternal life with God. However, do we know what are we saved for?

Destiny, purpose and *calling*—these are terms that are used commonly in the lives of believers, especially in these contemporary times. In the matter of choices, it is not about what we cannot do, or even what we have to do (religious obligation); rather, it is what we get to do.

Finding my own purpose for life was a radical process orchestrated by the Lord Himself. Because of my circumstances, there were a lot of things that had to be established foundationally before I could know or engage in my purpose. I think it is more important to really understand who you are than to understand what you are supposed to do.

Some people spend their whole lives working without really knowing their true identity. Find your identity by studying the life of the Lord Jesus.

Even as a twelve-year-old boy, Jesus showed surprising wisdom when sitting before the leaders in the Temple. He had been separated from His parents for three days after a visit to Jerusalem. Upon locating her son, His mother, Mary, asked Him why He had done this. She told Him that she and Joseph had been searching frantically for Him. His response was, "Did you not know that I must be about My Father's business?" (Luke 2:49).

His identity was in His relationship with God as Father, as well as in understanding the business for which He was sent. However, for the next eighteen years, Jesus lived with His parents in their home and community. There He grew to manhood—in wisdom and stature—and found favor with God and men before launching His ministry (see Luke 2:52).

My Father Speaks Purpose to Me

Scripture records three times that witnesses observed the Father speaking audibly with Jesus. The first was at His baptism when the

Father said, "This is My beloved Son, in whom I am well pleased" (Matthew 3:17).

In this first encounter, Jesus heard incredible prophetic affirmation from the Father, even when He had not yet done any preaching or miracles. This affirmation was based on relationship and not on performance.

The second time the Father spoke from heaven was when Jesus took Peter, James and John up a mountain to pray. As the three disciples were waking from a heavy sleep, they saw Jesus transfigured with Moses on one side of Him and Elijah on the other. In typical Peter fashion, the brash disciple spoke up, not knowing what he was really asking.

> "Lord, it is good for us to be here; if You wish, let us make here three tabernacles: one for You, one for Moses, and one for Elijah." While he was still speaking, behold, a bright cloud overshadowed them; and suddenly a voice came out of the cloud, saying, "This is My beloved Son, in whom I am well pleased. Hear Him!"
>
> Matthew 17:4–5

In this second encounter, Peter, James and John witnessed an astounding supernatural revelation of Jesus. Moses and Elijah were standing with Him, conversing about His departure from the earth. Having a skin-deep understanding about what was happening and a tendency toward reactivity, Peter wants to build monuments for each of them. As a cloud shrouds them, the Father makes a bold declaration: "Don't react to the supernatural with your own intention or purpose. Just listen to Jesus. This is the key to purpose."

The third encounter occurs as Jesus declares His feelings.

> "Now My soul is troubled, and what shall I say? 'Father, save Me from this hour'? But for this purpose I came to this hour. Father, glorify your name."
>
> Then a voice came from heaven, saying, "I have both glorified it and will glorify it again."

Therefore the people who stood by and heard it said that it had thundered. Others said, "An angel has spoken to Him."

John 12:27–29

I would like to believe and interpret the Father's response as saying, "I'm going to glorify My name again and again and again . . . forever—through You and through other sons and daughters who will come after You!"

It is on the basis of the Father-Son relationship that purpose is understood. I believe this is the priority for all sons and daughters in God's Kingdom. You are one of God's children and are called according to His purposes. He is not ashamed to call you brethren. You are accepted in the Beloved, and you bring Him pleasure because you are His own. This powerful insight needs to be your own personal revelation and spiritual encounter.

Everything about my life was lost or altered the moment the airplane crashed that summer day. Although I was raised in the church, I was not an authentic believer. I did not even know what one was. My identity was in how I looked, what I could do, how I could perform in front of people and what that would provide for me.

What I gained after my extraordinary entrance into the third heaven was eternal life. My new life, however, was confined to a ravaged body that was missing all the former amenities I had previously enjoyed. My purpose, after surviving the "unsurvivable," was continued healing and restoration from issues that required the miraculous hand of God. In those years of healing and restoration, I required a great deal of sovereign Holy Spirit teaching and equipping for His purposes.

When I was no longer in intensive care yet still facing a lot of big operations in the years following, an unanswered question continued to nag me.

What am I supposed to do now?

In that era—the late '60s and early '70s—the music scene and pop culture were littered with all types of influences to attract and entice, including free love, antiwar, the peace movement and "if it feels good do it," which was heralded by so-called truth seekers.

For some people, including me, there was the epic revelatory experience of learning that truth is a person. Jesus' declared that the same love the Father has for us would be manifested in us in His personal presence (see John 17).

As we come to know Jesus we also come into relationship with our heavenly Father, and we experience the activity of the indwelling of the Holy Spirit.

Although being called into the ministry required some adjustment, I see now that it is what I was created for, what I have been equipped for and what I most enjoy doing. The priority must always be relationship first, then doing His work in its own proper time and place. Coming from such a broken and humble beginning, who could have known that I would travel all over the world carrying this message? There were circumstances, people, places and things that all had to connect to make this pilgrimage possible. Much of it did not make sense at the time. It does truly require supernatural courage to go the distance.

Will We Finish Well?

Let us look at Moses. He was delivered from the sword of slaughter at his birth, he was raised in Egypt and he discovered his identity and fled Egypt. At the burning bush, he encountered the Lord dramatically. At that time, he heard the Lord communicate his impossible assignment. The conclusion of this prophetic assignment was to deliver God's people and bring them into the Promised Land. All of these things required unparalleled spiritual bravery. Even though Moses led the people all of the way to the Promised

Land, he could not go in. By his own mistake—an outburst of anger—he was prevented from going the distance.

Another spiritual giant was Elijah. Elijah the Tishbite was like a linebacker on God's team with an overdose of courage. He performed sixteen earth-shattering miracles, including stopping and starting rain after three and a half years, walking across a dry riverbed after he struck the ground to divide the waters, and defeating the prophets of Baal on Mount Carmel by pouring water on a sacrifice and then calling fire down to burn it up (see 1 Kings and 2 Kings). A successful ministry, wouldn't you think?

Yet, in spite of this, Elijah ran away from the threat of Jezebel and hid in a cave. He became overwhelmed by the fear that he was the only one serving God (see 1 Kings 19). Have you known anybody who felt like this?

When confronting the prophet, the first question the Lord asks is, "What are you doing here, Elijah?" (1 Kings 19:9). In other words, the Lord was asking why Elijah had left his calling. The Lord tells him to anoint two people to oversee the kingdoms and to anoint Elisha to take his place. This was seemingly an abrupt end to a heroic ministry of spiritual bravery. God cut Elijah's ministry and purpose short because of his fear and isolation.

Is it true that two of God's finest, Moses and Elijah, did not make it to the finish line? But that is not the end of the story . . . stay tuned.

Fantastic Finishes

Flash-forward about a half-dozen centuries into the ministry of our Lord. Peter, the oldest disciple; John, the youngest; and James, who would have the shortest amount of time in ministry before he was martyred, are privileged to be in Jesus' inner circle. Why did Jesus invest in these three men and call them to be part of some very special events in His personal life and ministry?

Let's revisit the glorious story in Luke 9:28–36, where Jesus takes Peter, James and John up to the mountain to pray. The three apostles are awakened from a deep sleep to see the glorified Jesus conversing with Moses (who represented the Law) and Elijah (who represented the prophets). They are asking Him when He is going to finish His earthly ministry.

As I was reading this story one day, God revealed to me that this is actually how the stories of Moses and Elijah ended. This is how Moses got to enter the Promised Land, and how Elijah did not end his time of ministry isolated in a cave. During His earthly ministry, Jesus set right the narrative that Moses and Elijah were supposed to have had. Moses got to go the distance because of Jesus, and Elijah was no longer isolated in a cave dreading his possible end at the hands of a wicked woman. Both men ended up on a mountaintop prophetically representing their ministries with Jesus before three awestruck disciples.

Peter draws powerful attention to this event in his second epistle:

> Yes, I think it is right, as long as I am in this tent, to stir you up by reminding you, knowing that shortly I must put off my tent, just as our Lord Jesus Christ showed me. . . . [We] were eyewitnesses of His majesty . . . when we were with Him on the holy mountain.
>
> 2 Peter 1:13–18

Remember, too, that Peter appeared to fall short by denying Jesus three times. He did not even consider himself worthy to be called a disciple. In spite of his weaknesses, Jesus restored Peter and allowed this feisty disciple to go the distance.

Tips to Keep Going Strong

A story goes that an older prophetic man of God who was always fresh, expectant and full of fire was asked how he maintained his zeal after so many years. With a mischievous smile on his face, the older man replied, "I've never lost the wonder of it all!"

- **Remain childlike.** It is an amazing thing not to become desensitized to the awesomeness of God. Be someone who says, "Wow! I wonder what the Lord is going to do next. I want to be right up front to see it."
- **Celebrate whenever you see the Lord doing something in someone else.** Life-hardened people can become critical and jealous. Joyful, thankful people are expectant— zealous instead of jealous.
- **Write the vision.** Many people write mission statements that serve as personal maps that project what they want to accomplish throughout their lives.
- **Record, remember and recite any and all personal prophecies, dreams and visions** that you know to be true about you and those with whom you walk. The Spirit magnifies and personalizes preaching and teaching for your edification and guidance.
- **Learn to perceive and recognize the touches of God.** You can start to recognize His fingerprints on people and events in your life. Your senses will grow sharper the more you understand these things.
- **Be prepared for change.** Every move of God has had unique characteristics. Some might say, "But that can't be God. That's not the way He did it when . . ." Jesus once spoke a parable to the Pharisees who had questioned Him as to why His disciples did not fast as their own disciples did. He replied, "Nor do they put new wine into old wineskins, or else the wineskins break, the wine is spilled, and the wineskins are ruined" (Matthew 9:17). The joy of the redemptive message of Jesus cannot be contained in legalistic and ritualistic doctrine that is void of the life of

the Spirit. The Passover Supper, for example, had been celebrated fervently for fifteen hundred years, but the night before He suffered, Jesus turned it into the Lord's Supper/Communion. We are instructed to do the same, remembering Him, our Lord and Savior, and celebrating the redemption purchased by Him in the New Covenant.

Tenacity in Staying the Course

During a very dangerous and arduous journey, Paul testifies before King Agrippa concerning his life and ministry. After describing his previous life as a persecutor of the Church, he begins to unfold this astounding spiritual encounter: "At midday, O king, along the road I saw a light from heaven, brighter than the sun, shining around me and those who journeyed with me" (Acts 26:13).

In this encounter, Paul received an amazing call to minister before Gentiles, kings and the children of Israel. "Therefore, King Agrippa, I was not disobedient to the heavenly vision, but declared . . . that they should repent, turn to God, and do works befitting repentance" (verses 19–20). He later states, "'King Agrippa, do you believe the prophets? I know that you do believe.' Then Agrippa said to Paul, 'You almost persuade me to become a Christian'" (verses 27–28). Although his life was at stake, Paul's purpose was to share the truth about Jesus. Instead of adversity, he saw opportunity.

Despite warnings through various prophecies that he would be bound, arrested and persecuted on his journey to Jerusalem, Paul pressed on. Some of his friends even begged him to stay with them. Yet, when they realized he could not be persuaded from staying the course, they said, "The will of the Lord be done" (Acts 21:14).

True to their prophecy, Paul was arrested in the city. Amid tumultuous confrontations and even secret plots to kill him, he continued with holy boldness to preach about Jesus. Should he not have considered all of the warnings to avoid this? Could he have doubted his own discernment and perception and tried to protect himself? Tension in the city was so heightened that even the military commander was afraid that the people might tear Paul to pieces.

But Paul remained tenacious in his determination to stand firm for his Lord. The following night he received more than a confirmation. Jesus stood by him and said, "Be of good cheer, Paul; for as you have testified for Me in Jerusalem, so you must also bear witness at Rome" (Acts 23:11). To have the courage to go the distance, we need to make a commitment not to turn back.

Commitment is like skydiving. Deciding to jump and putting on a parachute is one level of commitment. Getting in an airplane and taking a position—"It will be my turn next"—is another level of commitment. Jumping out of an open door of the airplane? Now that is what commitment is really all about.

Like Paul, I want to be able to testify that "I have fought the good fight, I have finished the race, I have kept the faith" (2 Timothy 4:7).

The Last Run

While visiting our son Matthew; his wife, Natasha; and our beautiful grandson, Solomon, in California at the end of January, I had a nice surprise visit with the Lord. It happened while I was snow skiing. I really love skiing, and I have always been pretty aggressive. Well, maybe not quite as aggressive as I was when I was younger.

For the first couple of days, my son Matt skied with me. But on the last day of my visit, he could not leave Natasha alone with the baby. I set out by myself for the ski run. With nobody there in this winter wonderland, I skied several times, enjoying the sting of the cold air on my face. Glancing at my watch, I realized that I had time for one more run before heading back to the house.

As I was riding up in the lift, I looked down on the terrain below, trying to figure out my turns. When you know it is going to be the last time, you really want to make it a pretty flashy run. But that is also the run where most injuries occur. Often at that time of day the light is flat, and it is harder to see. Though your mind is sharp and you know what you are doing, your muscles are a little tired. They might not be able to pull it out if you catch an edge. I wanted to make this last run a good one.

It was then that the Holy Spirit came upon me, real and close—as penetrating as the sharp mountain air. I slid out of the ski lift chair and stood on top of the hill gazing at the scene below. With the fading sunlight filtering through the trees, the setting was surreal.

I tightened the top latches on my ski boots and defogged my goggles, taking a mental snapshot of the downhill slope. I divided the run into three sections. I saw myself lunging off the headwall and carving a turn from left to right to get my skis gliding smoothly. Crossing over the middle of the run the hill dropped off into a steep angle. There, tall trees lined the slope and cast long shadows over the course—great for skiing, but also able to conceal certain dangers. I would keep my skis tightly parallel and dance down the terrain with hip-swinging rhythm, leaving a track of back-and-forth *S* turns. For the last third of that run, I could see an opening in the tree line that connected to the next downhill course on the right. I would cut through that opening, hit that first mogul, catch some air in a tuck position and then ski freely on the long stretch to the bottom of the hill.

It occurred to me that this pattern was much like my life. At the top of the run, I embraced the challenge to share my newfound faith with boldness and rising courage. I hit my stride about midway through taking the twists and turns, avoiding hidden traps and empowered by the Spirit flowing freely through me. Now, facing the last stretch, I will "catch some air" for the final burst of speed to cross the finish line.

The Lord showed me that the last run is like those defining moments in life—moments when you realize that your ministry is changing and that this may be the final opportunity to accomplish whatever He has given you to do. Joy bubbled up from within as the Lord impressed upon me that my last run may take at least 20 or 25 years to complete. I was overwhelmed with gratitude for what

I have been able to do in the Lord, but also for how much more I expect from Him in the time I have in front of me.

By the way, I did have a really good run and went down the hill pretty fast. But what I expect to experience in the days and years ahead fills me with an exhilaration that exceeds anything I have experienced previously. As Jesus said to Paul, "Be of good cheer [be courageous, be spiritually brave]! I'm not through with you yet! I've been able to take you this far, and I always finish what I start" (see Acts 23:11).

Your future is now. Your strength to run is in Him. Seize what our Lord has laid out for you. Go the distance and finish well.

MEDITATION: Bible Promises for Courage to Go the Distance

Abraham breathed his last and died in a good old age, an old man and full of years, and was gathered to his people.

Genesis 25:8

Jesus said to them, "My food is to do the will of Him who sent Me, and to finish His work."

John 4:34

I have no greater joy than to hear that my children walk in truth.

3 John 1:4

For further reading: Acts 20:26–27.

PRAYER for Courage to Go the Distance

O gracious Father, I honor You for Your faithfulness to care and provide wisely all these days of my life. "You compre-hend my path and my lying down, and are acquainted with all my ways. . . . How precious also are Your thoughts to me, O God! How great is the sum of them" (Psalm 139:3, 17).

Father, I am aware that You desire to lead and guide me in every major and minor decision, and I thank You in advance. I remember and declare that Jesus said that the glory He was given He is now giving to us, His followers and true disciples. Lord, I ask that You give me strength in the inner man—in my heart and mind. I also ask that my body would be renewed so that I can serve You all the days of my life. Lord, I ask for increased opportunities to influence people to partake in Your harvest. Finally, Lord, I ask that You give me wisdom to walk in Your ways and to be at peace. In Jesus' name, Amen.

ACTIVATION

- Write a mission statement that will be a personal road map for the future—not a bucket list but a desired destiny declaration. Keep in mind this statement should be adjustable, always making room for something better that the Lord might show you.

- Consider the times and the seasons in your life that are still before you. What would you like to change to make more room for the Lord to use you as you go the distance?

DECLARATION

I declare that with God's help I will walk in His ways, keep the faith, go the distance and finish well.

NOTES

Chapter 1: Courage to Hope

1. Interestingly, many decades later, Independence would be the home training center of world-superstar basketball player Lebron James. As a hero of hope in the sports world, Lebron would lead his team, the Cavaliers, to break Cleveland's 52-year drought of having no professional championship in any sport. In accomplishing this feat, he brought hope to an entire city.

Chapter 3: Courage to Be Humble

1. Francis Frangipane, *The Three Battlegrounds: An In-Depth View of the Three Arenas of Spiritual Warfare: The Mind, the Church and the Heavenly Places* (Cedar Rapids, Iowa: Arrow, 2006), 21.

Chapter 4: Courage to Fight

1. John Blake, "She Survived a Standoff with a Gunman—Could You?," CNN, February 25, 2014, https://www.cnn.com/2014/02/22/us/tuff-survivor-gunman/index.html.

2. *Tell Me More* staff, "How One Woman's Faith Stopped a School Shooting," NPR, January 31, 2014, https://www.npr.org/2014/01/31/268417580/how-one-womans-faith-stopped-a-school-shooting.

3. Ibid.

4. Matt Smith, "Georgia School Shooting: Antoinette Tuff Hailed as Hero," CNN, August 23, 2013, https://www.cnn.com/2013/08/22/us/georgia-school-shooting-hero/index.html.

Chapter 6: Courage to Persevere

1. Reimar Schultze, *I Am Love* (Kokomo, Ind.: CTO Books, 2006), xi–xii.
2. Ibid., vii.

3. Leslie Toke, "Flagellants," *The Catholic Encyclopedia*, Vol. 6, accessed April 2013, http://www.newadvent.org/cathen/06089c.htm.

4. James Swan, "Luther: Sleeping in the Snow?" *Beggars All Reformation*, September 24, 2011, https://beggarsallreformation.blogspot.com/search ?q=sleeping+in+the+snow.

5. Joseph Pearce, "Solzhenitsyn: The Courage to Be a Christian," *Crisis Magazine*, December 18, 2012, https://www.crisismagazine.com/2012/solzhenitsyn-the -courage-to-be-a-christian.

Chapter 7: Courage to Use Spiritual Gifts

1. Michael Davis, "John Wimber: When Do We Get to Do the Stuff?" *Charismatica*, February 17, 2009, http://www.charismatica.com/2009/02/17/john-wimber-when -do-we-get-to-do-the-stuff/.

Chapter 9: Courage to Forgive

1. R. T. Kendall, *Total Forgiveness*, rev. and updated ed. (Lake Mary, Fla.: Charisma, 2007), 1–8.

2. R. T. Kendall, "Total Forgiveness," *Blog*, R. T. Kendall Ministries, accessed January 6, 2020, https://rtkendallministries.com/total-forgiveness-2.

Chapter 10: Courage to Love

1. Richard Wurmbrand, *Tortured for Christ* (Barlesville, Okla.: Living Sacrifice Book, 1967), 67.

2. James Kiefer, "Laurence, Deacon and Martyr," *Justus Anglican*, http:// justus.anglican.org/resources/bio/223.html.

Chapter 11: Courage to Go the Distance

1. I believe that you would really enjoy reading Don's books. They are: *Your People Shall Be My People: How Israel, the Jews and the Christian Church Will Come Together in the Last Days*; *God's Promise and the Future of Israel: Compelling Questions People Ask About Israel and the Middle East*; and *The Handbook for the End Times: Hope, Help and Encouragement for Living in the Last Days*.

As a nineteen-year-old professional skydiver, **Mickey Robinson** underwent a plane crash that left him with catastrophic injuries: massive third-degree burns on half his body, lacerations, head trauma and blindness in his right eye. After this near-death experience, Mickey courageously overcame multiple terminal medical complications and recovered miraculously, as documented in his memoir *Falling into Heaven*. Since his second chance at life, Mickey has been a public speaker nationally and internationally, sharing words of encouragement and hope that continue to change lives and inspire people of all ages. Mickey and his wife live outside of Franklin, Tennessee. Learn more at www.mickeyrobinson.com.